DINOSAURS

igloobooks

igloobooks

Published in 2015
by Igloo Books Ltd
Cottage Farm
Sywell
NN6 0BJ
www.igloobooks.com

All images supplied courtesy of HL Studios

SHE001 0615
2 4 6 8 10 9 7 5 3
ISBN 978-1-78197-591-6

Printed and manufactured in China

CONTENTS

Interactive Instructions

On your mobile, or tablet device, download the **FREE** Layar App.

Look out for the **SCAN ME** logo and scan the whole page.

Unlock, discover and enjoy the enhanced content.

For more details, visit: **www.igloobooks.com**

INTRODUCTION

The world we live in today will change in your lifetime, and if you ask your parents and grandparents, they will tell you how much it has changed in their lifetime. Humans have spread across Earth and we have colonized and visited virtually all of the land mass available on our planet. We are continuing to explore to the very bottom of our oceans and even beyond our own planet. We have explored our Moon and now we are beginning to explore other planets such as Mars, Venus and beyond.

Although it is true that we humans have had phenomenal success during our time on Earth, it is also true that Earth is a lot, lot older than us. Our time on Earth is absolutely tiny compared to the total amount of time there has been life on Earth.

Earth is about 4.5 billion years old, but humans have lived on Earth for only the last 200,000 years. Let's put it another way. Stretch out your arm and fingers, then look at the length of your arm from your shoulder all the way to your fingers. The very tip of the fingernail on your longest finger represents how long humans have been on Earth. If you take a nail file and scrape off the tip of that fingernail, then you have just wiped out the existence of humans on planet Earth.

Although they became extinct about 65 million years ago, dinosaurs lived on Earth for about 165 million years. That is a far greater amount of time than we have lived on Earth so far. If you stretch out your arm again, the time that the dinosaurs lived on Earth would be about the length of your middle finger.

Our planet looked very different then. It had one large land mass (or continent) called Pangaea.

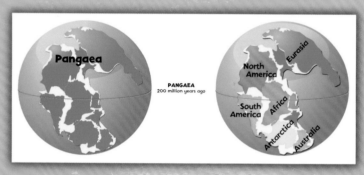

PANGAEA
200 million years ago

Because dinosaurs died out a long time ago, our knowledge of them can only be gained from the fossils we've found. Advances in modern technology, such as MRI scans and high-powered X-rays, have revealed much more information about the fossils we have already discovered, as have advances in our studies of animal and reptile behaviour.

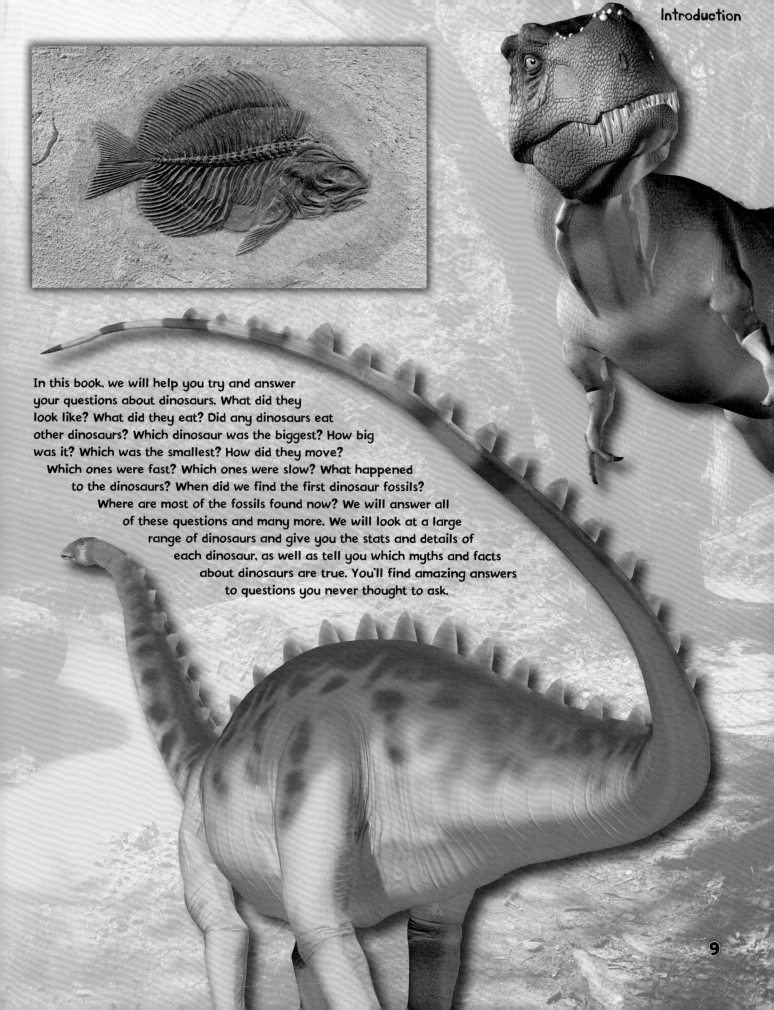

In this book, we will help you try and answer
your questions about dinosaurs. What did they
look like? What did they eat? Did any dinosaurs eat
other dinosaurs? Which dinosaur was the biggest? How big
was it? Which was the smallest? How did they move?
Which ones were fast? Which ones were slow? What happened
to the dinosaurs? When did we find the first dinosaur fossils?
Where are most of the fossils found now? We will answer all
of these questions and many more. We will look at a large
range of dinosaurs and give you the stats and details of
each dinosaur, as well as tell you which myths and facts
about dinosaurs are true. You'll find amazing answers
to questions you never thought to ask.

DINOSAUR TIMELINE

FIRST DINOSAURS
230 million years ago
The first dinosaurs evolve.
They are mostly small, no more
than 6 m (20 ft), bipedal and
fast moving. Marine reptiles
such as Icthyosaurs and
Plesiosaurs, also evolve
at this time.

VOLCANOES ERUPT
248 million years ago
Massive volcanic eruptions
cause global extinctions,
wiping out 90% of marine
life and 70% of land life!

FIRST MAMMALS
206-144 million years ago
Dinosaurs dominant as the
first mammals evolve.

Mesozoic Era

248–65 million years ago

Triassic Period

248–206 million years ago

Jurassic Period

206–144 million years ago

Sauropsids such
as the archosaurs,
dominate and
the first
cynodonts evolve.

Eoraptor
Coelophysis

Stegosaurus

Compsognathus
Diplodocus
Brachiosaurus

Apatosaurus
Kentrosaurus
Seismosaurus
Allosaurus

Megalosaurus

AGE OF THE DINOSAURS
144-65 million years ago
Dinosaurs are at their peak
in size, variety and
numbers and dominate
every continent.

EXTINCTION
65 million years ago
The K-T (Creataceous-Tertiary)
extinction causes the end of the
dinosaurs dominance.

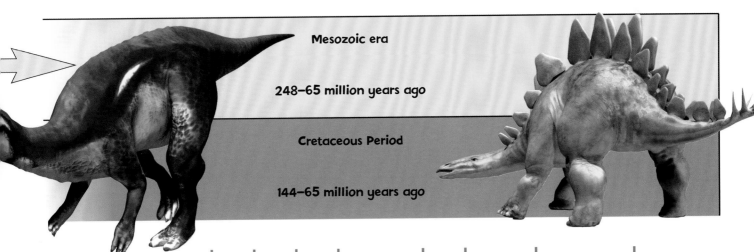

Mesozoic era

248–65 million years ago

Cretaceous Period

144–65 million years ago

Hadrosaurus
Velociraptor
Protoceratops

Centrosaurus
Troodon
Tyrannosaurus
Triceratops
Ankylosaurus
Edmontosaurus

Giganotosaurus
Spinosaurus

Argentinosaurus
Nodosaurus

Deinonychus

Acrocanthosaurus

Iguanodon

Baryonyx

ERYOPS

Eryops was one of the largest animals of its time, measuring 1.5–2.0 m (5–6 ft) long. It lived roughly 270 million years ago, during the Permian period. A fierce amphibian, it might have resembled a modern-day alligator.

SUPER FACT

Eryops had primitive ears which allowed it to hear airborne sounds.

DID YOU KNOW?

Eryops (AR-ee-ops) was named in 1887 by Edward Drinker Cope, an American scientist.

GUESS WHAT?

Eryops was a meat-eater. It had thick, strong bones, four powerful legs and a short tail. It moved very slowly on land because of its bulky body and short legs. *Eryops* ate mostly fish, small reptiles and other amphibians.

WOW, REALLY?

Eryops grabbed prey in its powerful jaws, then threw its head up and tossed the meat backwards and deep into its mouth.

DiMETRODON

Dimetrodon was a sail-backed, meat-eating animal that lived during the Permian period, roughly 280 million years ago. When *Dimetrodon* was alive, deserts covered much of Earth and it was perfectly suited to living in hot, dry conditions. *Dimetrodon* was believed to be very fierce and had no predators. Fossilized skeletons indicate that this creature could be as big as 3.5 m (11.5 ft) long and probably weighed about 250 kg (550lbs). *Dimetrodon* walked on four legs, which sprawled out to the sides. It is likely to have been a very fast runner.

SAIL BACK

The *Dimetrodon* used its distinctive sail to soak up valuable sunlight during the daytime to control the heat of its body. It was also used to ward off other species.

HOW DO YOU SAY MY NAME?

DIE-met-ruh-don

WOW, AMAZING!

Dimetrodon had two types of teeth. Long teeth at the front to cut through meat and shorter ones at the back to tear the meat into small pieces.

DID YOU KNOW?

Many people think that *Dimetrodon* was a dinosaur. However, *Dimetrodon* lived tens of millions of years before the first dinosaurs appeared on Earth. *Dimetrodon* is probably more closely related to humans than to dinosaurs. It is a pelycosaur, which had many mammal-like characteristics and is a relative of warm-blooded mammals.

EDAPHOSAURUS

Edaphosaurus was one of the earliest known plant-eaters. It got its name from living on land, as *Edaphosaurus* means 'earth lizard' in Greek. It looked similar to *Dimetrodon*, because of the sail on its back, although *Edaphosaurus* was smaller. This reptile lived roughly 320 million years ago. We still know very little about the *Edaphosaurus*, as the only fossils that have ever been found consisted of only a few fragments of its skeleton. We do know that *Edaphosaurus* lived in what is now known as North America and Western Europe.

FOUR LEGS

Edaphosaurus was a quadruped and was 3.2 m (11 ft) long and weighed about 300 kg (660 lbs).

TEMPERATURE CONTROL

If *Edaphosaurus* got too hot it would stand in a cooling breeze to cool down.

DID YOU KNOW?

Like the *Dimetrodon*, the *Edaphosaurus* was a pelycosaur. Pelycosaurs were small lizard-like animals that evolved into much larger and very different types.

AWESOME

Although *Edaphosaurus* could chew its food, it also had a very large gut, so it would swallow large amounts of partly chewed leaves and stems. They would ferment in its gut to release the nutrients.

TRIASSIC PERIOD

WHEN WAS THE TRIASSIC PERIOD?

The Triassic Period was the first part of the Mesozoic Era, the age of the dinosaurs. It lasted from around 248-206 million years ago. During the Triassic Period, dinosaurs and mammals evolved.

WHAT WAS THE CLIMATE LIKE?

The Triassic climate was generally hot and dry with strong seasons. The formation of the supercontinent of Pangaea, approximately 300 million years ago, decreased the amount of shoreline, formed mountains and gave the interior of the supercontinent a dry, desert-like terrain.

WHAT NO ICE?

The polar regions were moist and temperate and there was no polar ice.

DID YOU KNOW?

The Triassic Period was named in 1834 by the German geologist Friedrich August von Alberti (1795-1878). It was originally named the 'Trias'.

TRIASSIC ANIMALS AND PLANTS

There were no dinosaurs at the beginning of the Triassic Period, but there were many amphibians, some reptiles and dicynodonts. During the early Triassic Period, corals appeared, ammonites recovered from the Permian extinction and seed plants dominated the land. Also, about 220 million years ago, the first mammals appeared. Some scientists believe that mammals evolved from a group of extinct mammal-like reptiles. These primitive mammals were tiny and are thought to have been nocturnal. The very earliest dinosaurs were small, two-legged meat-eaters, such as *Coelophysis* (see page 44) and *Eoraptor* (see page 52). The rise of dinosaurs during the late Triassic Period led to the decline of other previously successful animal groups. Many reptiles and amphibians disappeared and so did advanced mammal-like reptiles.

VOLCANOES ERUPT

Although no one is certain wht caused the end of the Triassic Period, it is very likely it ended with a mass extinction accompanied by huge volcanic eruptions about 213–208 million years ago. Roughly 35% of all animal families died out. Most of the early primitive dinosaurs became extinct, but other more adaptive dinosaurs evolved in the Jurassic Period. This extinction allowed the dinosaurs to become increasingly dominant and remained that way for the next 150 million years.

DID YOU KNOW?

Turtles, frogs, salamanders and lizards (including snakes) all first appeared in the Triassic Period.

JURASSIC PERIOD

WHEN WAS THE JURASSIC PERIOD?

After the Triassic Period came the Jurassic Period, which lasted from 206–144 million years ago. Huge, long-necked dinosaurs appeared during the Jurassic Period.

SCAN ME
Instructions on page 5

DID YOU KNOW?

The Jurassic Period is named after rock strata found in the Jura Mountains, which are located between France and Switzerland.

WHAT WAS THE CLIMATE LIKE?

SUPER FACT

About 140 million years ago, during the late Jurassic Period, flowering plants evolved and would soon change the visible face of Earth.

At the beginning of the Jurassic Period, the climate was hot and dry. When Pangaea began to break up, it created large flooded areas, tropical forests and coral reefs. The break-up of the land created large seas that affected the global climate.

ANIMALS AND PLANTS IN THE JURASSIC

During the Jurassic Period, relatives of the plant-eating prosauropods of the Triassic Period evolved into gigantic sauropods, such as *Brachiosaurus* and *Diplodocus*. This period also saw the rise of medium- to large-sized theropod dinosaurs, such as *Allosaurus* and *Megalosaurus*, which helps explain the evolution of the earliest ankylosaurs, the armoured plant-eating dinosaurs. The Jurassic Period was also the heyday of the stegosaurs, typified by *Stegosaurus*.

Marine Life
Just as dinosaurs grew bigger on land, so did the marine reptiles of the Jurassic Period gradually attain gigantic proportions. The Jurassic seas were filled with fierce pliosaurs, such as *Liopleurodon*, as well as less frightening swimmers like *Plesiosaurus*. Prehistoric fish were abundant, as were squid and prehistoric sharks, providing a steady source of nourishment for these and other marine reptiles.

Avian Life
By the end of the Jurassic Period, the skies were filled with relatively advanced pterosaurs, such as *Pteranodon* and *Dimorphodon*.

Plant Life
Gigantic herbivorous dinosaurs such as *Brachiosaurus* and *Diplodocus* could not have evolved if they did not have a reliable source of food. The lands of the Jurassic Period had lots of tasty vegetation, including ferns, conifers, cycads, club mosses and horsetails.

WHAT HAPPENED TO THE JURASSIC PERIOD?

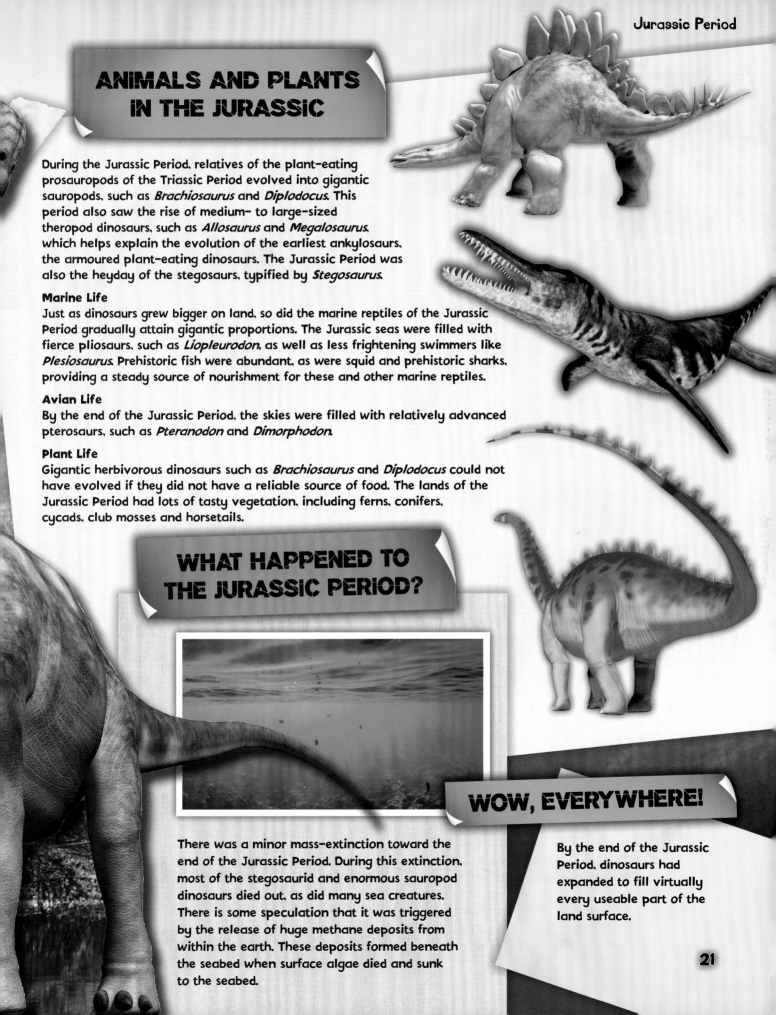

There was a minor mass-extinction toward the end of the Jurassic Period. During this extinction, most of the stegosaurid and enormous sauropod dinosaurs died out, as did many sea creatures. There is some speculation that it was triggered by the release of huge methane deposits from within the earth. These deposits formed beneath the seabed when surface algae died and sunk to the seabed.

WOW, EVERYWHERE!

By the end of the Jurassic Period, dinosaurs had expanded to fill virtually every useable part of the land surface.

21

CRETACEOUS PERIOD

WHEN WAS THE CRETACEOUS PERIOD?

After the Jurassic Period came the Cretaceous Period. This lasted from 144–65 million years ago. This was the last part of the Mesozoic Era and most known dinosaurs lived during this period.

DID YOU KNOW?

Creta is the Latin word for chalk. The Cretaceous Period is named after the chalky rock from south-eastern England that was the first Cretaceous Period sediment studied.

$$2 + 2 = 4$$

WHAT WAS THE CLIMATE LIKE?

During the early Cretaceous Period, the break-up of the Pangaean supercontinent into smaller continents continued, with the first outlines of modern North and South America, Europe, Asia and Africa taking shape. Conditions were hot and humid like the Jurassic Period, with the added twist of rising sea levels and the spread of endless swamps. This created an ecological environment in which dinosaurs and other prehistoric life could flourish.

SUPER FACT

Flowers, flowering trees and grasses became more and more common during the Cretaceous Period, helped along by the evolution of bees that carried pollen from one flower to another. By the end of the Cretaceous Period, most of the plants on Earth were flowering ones.

CRETACEOUS PLANTS AND ANIMALS

During the Cretaceous Period, dinosaurs really came into their own. Thousands of dinosaurs roamed the slowly separating continents, including Raptors and Tyrannosaurs. There were also other varieties of theropods, including ornithomimids (bird mimics) and lots of small, feathered dinosaurs, including the very intelligent *Troodon*. The classic sauropods of the Jurassic Period had pretty much died out, but their descendants, the lightly armoured titanosaurs, spread to every continent on Earth. Ceratopsians, horned, frilled dinosaurs, such as *Styracosaurus and Triceratops*, also became abundant.

Marine Life
Shortly after the beginning of the Cretaceous Period, the ichthyosaurs (fish lizards) left the scene, and were replaced by mosasaurs, gigantic pliosaurs such as *Kronosaurus*, and slightly smaller plesiosaurs, such as *Elasmosaurus*.

Avian Life
By the end of the Cretaceous Period, the pterosaurs, such as *Quetzalcoatlus*, had finally attained the enormous sizes of their cousins on land and in the sea. However, the pterosaurs were gradually crowded out of the sky by the first real prehistoric birds, which evolved from land-dwelling, feathered dinosaurs, not pterosaurs.

WOW FACT!

The earliest fossils of birds resembling pelicans, flamingoes and sandpipers were from the Cretaceous Period.

WHAT HAPPENED TO THE CRETACEOUS?

At the end of the Cretaceous Period, about 65 million years ago, a mass extinction wiped out the dinosaurs and many other animals. The primary cause of the extinction is thought to be an asteroid impact on the Yucatan Peninsula that raised huge clouds of dust, blotting out the sun and causing most of this vegetation to die out. However, there are also lots of other theories for this extinction, including volcanoes erupting and climate change owing to continental drift. The age of dinosaurs came to an end; the age of mammals was about to begin.

DINOSAUR BRAINS

For a long time, palaeontologists have considered dinosaurs to be stupid creatures with small brains and little intelligence. However, that view is changing. By studying the brains of other animals, we can compare the intelligence they display alongside the size of their brains to tell use more about dinosaurs. Intelligence does not always mean you have to have a big brain. The environment you live in plays a part, too. For example, if dinosaurs chewed plants all day, they wouldn't need a very big brain to process what they needed to know. However, they should still be considered intelligent, because all the information they needed to process on a daily basis was contained within a small brain.

WOW, REALLY?

Stegosaurus would have weighed around 3 tons and had a brain the same size as a walnut.

IS THAT TRUE?

The brain is an organ so it is one of the first parts of the body to rot away. This means palaeontologists use fossilized skulls to make hypotheses about dinosaur brains.

BRAIN STATS

	10%	20%	30%	40%

A human brain weight is 2.5% of the overall body weight — **2.5%**

A rat's brain is 0.85% — **0.85%**

A dog's brain is 2.5% — **2.5%**

A sparrow's brain is 4.2% — **4.2%**

A *Diplodocus* brain is 0.001% — **0.001%**

AND THE WINNER IS... 1

...*Troodon*, a member of the theropoda family from the Cretaceous Period. The *Troodon* was the same height as a human, had large eyes that gave it stereo vision and was very fast. Palaeontologists believe that *Troodon* had a 'big' brain and when compared to its body weight, the *Troodon*'s brain size was way ahead of other dinosaurs.

DID YOU KNOW?

Troodon means 'wounding tooth' and it got this name from the sharp serrated tooth it had for ripping up meat.

HEADS AND TAILS

Every dinosaur was made up of similar skeletons. However, basic body parts such as their heads and tails, had very different appearances and functions. Sizes of heads and tails varied greatly across the various species of dinosaur. Studies of dinosaurs' skulls have given scientists lots of important information about the lifestyle and intelligence of dinosaurs.

HEAD FACTS

The biggest dinosaurs often had very small heads. A 30 ton *Brachiosaurus* may have needed to eat up to a ton of plants every day just to stay alive. However, it had a head not much larger than a horse and teeth that couldn't chew!

USE YOUR HEAD

Dinosaur skulls differed from dinosaur to dinosaur depending on what they were needed for. *Deinonychus* (see page 36) had a lightweight skull, while *Tyrannosaurus rex* (see page 30) had a large skull, which was heavily reinforced with bone and shock-absorbing muscle to withstand the impact of crashing into its victims.

TAIL FACTS

Like heads, dinosaurs' tails varied according to use. *Ankylosaurus* (see page 110) had a heavily armoured tail. *Ankylosaurus*, if attacked, could use its club-like tail as a weapon, swinging it from side to side like a knight's mace.

IT WASN'T ALWAYS EASY!

Scientists occasionally got it wrong. Here are two famous mix-ups:

ELASMOSAURUS WITH ITS HEAD ON ITS TAIL

In 1868, palaeontologist Edward Drinker Cope reconstructed an *Elasmosaurus* skeleton with its head on its tail. The error was quickly pointed out in a very unfriendly manner by Cope's rival, Othniel C Marsh, and the dispute escalated into what we now know as the 'Bone Wars'.

STEGOSAURUS WITH A BRAIN IN ITS BOTTOM!

However, Othniel Marsh made a mistake of his own. When *Stegosaurus* was first discovered in 1877, he thought it had a second brain in its bottom. Today, it is believed that *Stegosaurus* did not have two brains and the cavity in *Stegosaurus*' tail was used to store extra food.

SENSES

It is hard to tell what dinosaurs were like, because we have never been able to observe how they behave. However, scientists can work out information about their senses from the evidence left behind and by studying the behaviour and senses of animals that are around today.

TASTE FACTS

Scientists previously believed that plant-eating dinosaurs would have used taste to tell the difference between certain foods. However, some scientists now believe that plant-eaters may not have had a very good sense of taste after all, like modern-day reptiles. It is thought that they would not have been able to taste bitter poisons contained in some flowering plants evolving in the late Cretaceous Period and this may be one of the reasons they died out.

DEADLY

SIGHT FACTS

Most dinosaurs would have had good lateral vision, with eyes set at the sides of their heads, but since their eyes didn't face forward, they had difficulty judging distance. *Troodon* (see page 56) had exceptionally large eyes, based on the size of its eye sockets, and would have had very good vision. *Opthalmosaurus* had massive eyes, which would have helped it see in the dark, deep oceans – large eyes have more light-gathering cells and work really well in the dark.

SOUND FACTS

Dinosaurs did not have exterior ear flaps like mammals, but heard through holes set far back in the head behind their eyes. It was probably the 'herding' dinosaurs, with their strong need to communicate, that had the most acute sense of hearing. Hadrosaurs (see page 80) display the only real evidence so far of being able to make noises, with a variety of nasal trumpets and air sacs. It is likely dinosaurs would probably have made noises, if they needed to.

TOUCH FACTS

A dinosaur's sense of touch was probably not very well developed, because of their thick skin. However, there is some evidence to suggest *Velociraptor's* (see page 50) nose was very sensitive to touch!

SMELL FACTS

The meat-eating predators were probably able to smell very well, in order to hunt their prey. This evidence is based on the size and shape of their olfactory lobes (the parts of the brain linked to smell). *Tyrannosaurus rex* (see page 30) and *Giganotosaurus* (see page 32), the largest meat-eaters of all time, had a keen sense of smell and good eyesight. They could pick up the scent of dead bodies from a long distance, from which they could scavenge meat.

TYRANNOSAURUS REX

Tyrannosaurus rex means 'tyrant lizard king' and is one of the best-known dinosaurs. It lived during the Cretaceous Period and is one of the largest carnivores ever discovered. It could grow up to 12 m (39 ft) long – the size of a bus.

SCAN ME
Instructions on page 5

TYRANNOSAURUS STATS

NAME:	*Tyrannosaurus*
PRONUNCIATION:	ty-RAN-uh-SAWR-us
HEIGHT:	7 m (23 ft)
LENGTH:	12 m (39 ft)
DIET:	Meat – almost any other animal.
LIVED:	80-65 million years ago
FOSSILS FOUND:	North America and east Asia
PERIOD:	Upper Cretaceous
FEATURES:	Sharp teeth, each measuring 18-30 cm (7-12 in) long.

DINOSAUR SKIN

Although *Tyrannosaurus* is often pictured as being green, no-one actually knows if it was. Fossils don't give us any clues, so scientists look at modern-day animals, such as crocodiles and lizards, to help them guess what a dinosaur's scaly skin might have looked like.

EATING HABITS

Some experts think that *Tyrannosaurus* might have been a scavenger, rather than a hunter. Instead of hunting and killing prey themselves, scavengers find and eat animals that are already dead. Other scientists disagree, and it is one of the longest-running arguments in palaeontology.

FEARSOME TEETH

Tyrannosaurus' teeth were fixed into its gums, rather than its jawbone. This allowed new rows of teeth to grow underneath. When a tooth was lost, broken, or old, it fell out and a sharp, new one took its place.

GIGANOTOSAURUS

Giganotosaurus means 'giant southern lizard'. It lived at the same time as enormous, plant-eating dinosaurs such as the *Argentinosaurus*, which it hunted. A dominant predator, *Giganotosaurus* is the largest known meat-eater, even bigger than *Tyrannosaurus rex!* From its skull, which was over 1.8 m (6 ft), we know that it probably had a good sense of smell and its large eyes meant it had excellent eyesight.

WHAT A WHOPPER!

Giganotosaurus weighed the same as 125 people. It also hunted prey up to 10 times its own size!

NAME MIX-UP

The *Giganotosaurus* is not to be confused with another dinosaur called *Gigantosaurus* (different spelling), which is an African sauropod (giant, long-necked dinosaurs such as the *Diplodocus!* With only one letter difference in their names, you could easily get these two dinosaurs mixed up!

GIGANOTOSAURUS STATS

NAME:	*Giganotosaurus*
PRONUNCIATION:	JYE-ga-NO-toe-SAWR-us
HEIGHT:	5.5–7 m (18–23 ft)
LENGTH:	15 m (49 ft)
DIET:	Meat. Medium to very large animals.
LIVED:	100 million years ago
FOUND:	South America, mainly Argentina
PERIOD:	Early to middle Cretaceous Period
FEATURES:	Huge skull with sharp teeth.

WATCH THOSE FINGERS!

Giganotosaurus did not have the crushing bite of *Tyrannosaurus rex* and so would have attacked by slashing its victims with its three-taloned claws.

BANANA BRAIN

Giganotosaurus had a brain the shape and size of a banana, even though its skull was the size of a bathtub.

HOW BIG?

Look how *Giganotosaurus* compares to other dinosaurs. Pictured are (from small to large): *Compsognathus, Ornitholestes, Dilophosaurus, Torosaurus, Giganotosaurus* and *Camarasaurus*.

IT'S A GIANT

The biggest *Giganotosaurus* found was over a metre longer and a ton heavier than 'Sue', the largest known *Tyrannosaurus rex*.

33

HERRERASAURUS

Discovered in Argentina, Herrerasaurus means 'Herrera's lizard'. It was named after the rancher who discovered the first fossils — Victorino Herrera. *Herrerasaurus* was one of the earliest dinosaurs and lived during the Triassic Period. Despite its small size, *Herrerasaurus* was an active and very dangerous predator. It would have been a fast runner, had sharp teeth and its three-fingered hands were perfect for capturing prey.

NATURAL HUNTER

With its strong hind legs, short thighs and long feet, *Herrerasaurus* was a natural hunter. Fast and agile, it would hunt down and feast on prey using its large jaw and sharp teeth.

DISCOVERY FACT

The first skull of the *Herrerasaurus* was not found until 1988. This discovery, along with an almost complete skeleton, finally allowed palaeontologists to classify the dinosaur as a theropod.

HERRERASAURUS STATS

NAME:	*Herrerasaurus*
PRONUNCIATION:	her-RARE-uh-SAWR-us
HEIGHT:	1 m (3.3 ft)
LENGTH:	5 m (17 ft)
PERIOD:	Triassic Period

LIZARD-SIZED

Herrerasaurus was about the same length as the Komodo dragon, a giant lizard that lives today in Indonesia.

Dinosaurs

DEINONYCHUS

The name *Deinonychus* means 'terrible claw'. It was a carnivore and lived in the forests of what we now know as North America. *Deinonychus* lived in the middle Cretaceous Period, around 100 million years ago. *Deinonychus* was about 1.5 m (4 ft) tall, weighed about 80 kg (176 lbs) and measured 3 m (10 ft) from the tip of its nose to the end of its long, rigid tail. It had powerful jaws with sharp, jagged teeth. Its large head, compared to its body size, meant *Deinonychus* was one of the cleverest dinosaurs.

PACK HUNTING

Fossil evidence shows *Deinonychus* packs hunted and killed dinosaurs as much as 10 times their size, such as the *Tenontosaurus*.

SCAN ME
Instructions on page 5

36

JUMP ATTACK

Deinonychus' likely method of attack was to use its powerful back legs to leap into the air and land on its prey. It would dig its long, sickle toe-claws in, causing significant damage. It would then tear and bite its prey to cause as much blood loss as possible.

HUNTING TACTICS

The dromaeosauridae family all have quite large brains in comparison to their total body size, meaning they were some of the cleverest dinosaurs around. This would have allowed them to work together as a team and use simple tactics to guide their prey towards other members of the pack.

TERRIBLE CLAW

Deinonychus' second toe sported a vicious 13 cm (5 in) long claw, which is how it got its name. This claw could be held up out of the way when the creature was running, only snapping into position when needed for an attack. It was originally thought its long claw was used to slash prey, but recent studies have shown that it was probably used as a stabbing weapon, like a knife.

37

PROCOMPSOGNATHUS

Procompsognathus means 'before the elegant jaw'. It was alive during the late Triassic Period, around 210 million years ago. It lived in the swamps of what we now know as Western Europe. It was fast on its feet and caught insects, lizards, bugs and newly hatched reptiles to eat, chewing them up with its many small teeth. *Procompsognathus* walked upright on its long hind legs, balancing with its long, stiff, pointed tail, which it held off the ground. Its arms were short with large, four-fingered clawed hands, which it would have used for grabbing its prey.

NASTY BITE

It is believed that *Procompsognathus* could inflict a poisonous bite, although this has not been proved.

STILL A LOT TO FIND OUT

The poor quality of its fossil remains means we still do not know much about *Procompsognathus*. However, this small dinosaur was at the evolution base of the very successful family called theropoda.

WOW, FACT!

Procompsognathus was about the same weight as a pet cat, 1.8–3.2 kg (4–7 lbs), although it was much bigger in size and could grow up to 1.3 m (4 ft) long.

FOSSIL FACT!

Procompsognathus fossils have been discovered in Wittenberge, Germany. They were discovered by Eberhard Fraas in 1913.

CARCHARODONTOSAURUS

Nearly as large as *Tyrannosaurus rex*, this large meat-eater lived in what is now modern-day North Africa, 105–94 million years ago. It gets its name from the shark family and means 'sharp-toothed lizard'. *Carcharodontosaurus* lived in the middle Cretaceous Period and could weigh as much as four white rhinos.

ENVIRONMENT CHANGE

The environment is always changing owing to many factors including the Sun, volcanoes erupting and movements of the continents. North Africa is now dry and barren with many large sandy deserts. When the *Carcharodontosaurus* lived there, it was wet and hot with lots of plants, forests and animals, which made it good hunting grounds.

EWW GROSS!

While *Carcharodontosaurus* may have used its enormous jaw and many long, serrated teeth to hunt its prey, it would have also scavenged, eating rotting carcasses of dead animals.

CASUALTY OF WAR

Carcharodontosaurus fossils were first discovered in 1927 by Charles Deperet and J. Savornin in North Africa. Unfortunately, the first fossils were destroyed during World War II. Luckily, further fossils were subsequently found in North Africa by palaeontologist Paul Sereno in 1996.

LONG IN THE TOOTH

Carcharodontosaurus had long, sharp teeth that measured 20 cm (8 in). They also had one of the longest therapod skulls. One fossil found was 1.6 m (5 ft) long. However, *Giganotosaurus* had the biggest skull.

COMPSOGNATHUS

Compsognathus was one of the first complete dinosaur skeletons ever found. It is also one of the smallest, with a body about the size of a chicken and a head-to-tail length of around 1 m (3.3 ft). It lived in what is now France and Germany, during the late Jurassic Period. At that time, it would have been a tropical environment. *Compsognathus* was an early member of a group of dinosaurs called the coelurosaurs (hollow-tail lizards). Later coelurosaurs included the most likely ancestors of birds.

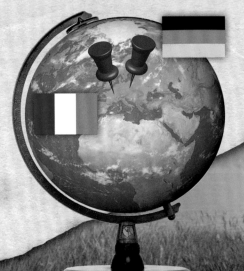

YOU'LL NEVER GUESS WHAT

At the time of this dinosaur, Europe was an archipelago, a series of tropical islands in the sea, like modern-day Indonesia.

SMALL BUT DEADLY

Compsognathus may have been small, but it was fast, agile and had very sharp teeth. The first fossil found in Germany had the remains of a lizard in its stomach cavity – its last meal before death. Have you ever tried to catch a lizard? Think of how fast you would have to be!

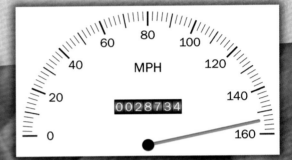

MOVIE STAR

Compsognathus featured throughout the dinosaur movie, *The Lost World: Jurassic Park*, where it hunted in large packs, overwhelming much larger prey than itself.

HOW MANY FINGERS?

Palaeontologists cannot agree over whether *Compsognathus* had two or three fingers on each hand. Either way, those slender fingers would have helped it grasp prey, which could then be swallowed whole or torn into pieces by its sharp teeth.

43

COELOPHYSIS

Coelophysis lived during the late Triassic Period, roughly 210 million years ago. *Coelophysis* is one of the earliest-known dinosaurs and was a meat-eater. Some think it may have also been a cannibal. It walked around on hind legs, in an upright position. *Coelophysis* lived in what was then a desert-like environment and its name refers to its hollow bones. *Coelophysis* is thought to have moved around and hunted in packs. Its teeth were like blades with fine, knife-like serrations, which suggests that it was a predatory dinosaur.

DINO WISH

An interesting fact about *Coelophysis* is that it had a wish bone, just like a chicken.

DID YOU KNOW?

Coelophysis, pronounced see-lo-FISE-iss, means 'hollow form', because it had hollow bones. This meant it was also very lightweight.

COELOPHYSIS THE CANNIBAL

Some scientists believe that Coelophysis were cannibals, because one fossil found had a baby Coelophysis in its stomach.

TO INFINITY AND BEYOND!

Coelophysis was the second dinosaur to go to space. Its skull was taken on-board the space shuttle Endeavor mission STS-89 in 1988.

AWESOME TAIL

Coelophysis used its tail as a counterweight when it was moving, so that it could keep its balance.

DROMAEOSAURUS

Dromaeosaurus was the first of a group of infamous dinosaurs to be discovered. The group was nicknamed 'raptors'. It lived in and around what is now north-western America and Canada, during the late Cretaceous Period. *Dromaeosaurus* means 'fast running lizard', however, this whole group of dinosaurs are believed to be closely related to birds.

PACK HUNTERS

Dromaeosaurus teeth have been found among the fossils of much larger dinosaurs. This suggests it hunted in packs, like wolves, so it could bring down much larger prey.

I BELIEVE I CAN FLY

Unfortunately *Dromaeosaurus* could not fly, however, some believe that its ancestors flew. They then became used to living on the ground so they grew bigger and stopped flying, like modern-day ostriches and emus. Also, some palaeontologists have suggested that these dinosaurs may have had colourful feathers from head to toe!

MINI-TYRANNOSAURUS?

With its deep, large jaw, short and massive skull and big strong teeth, *Dromaeosaurus* looks like a mini version of the *Tyrannosaurus rex*.

DEADLY WEAPONS

The *Dromaeosaurus* had lots of weapons and skills at its disposal:
- Sickle-shaped killing claws on hind feet, used for disembowelling prey.
- It was about 1.8 m (6 ft), large enough to pack a punch if it jumped onto its prey.
- It had very large eyes giving it good eyesight that helped it hunt.
- Many sharp and strong teeth in a long jaw meant it could not only tear the meat off its prey, but hang on and grapple them to the ground.
- Powerful hind legs allowed it to run at very fast speeds and jump high.
- A stiff and straight tail allowed it to balance while hunting prey, meaning it could be very agile across all sorts of terrain.

COELURUS

Coelurus was a small, well-adapted predator. It lived in what we now know as central and western USA, during the Jurassic Period. It hunted around swampy areas, eating frogs, lizards and insects. Its name comes from its hollow tail and most of what we know about *Coelurus* comes from a single skeleton.

WHO FOUND COELURUS

Coelurus was discovered by the famous dinosaur hunter, Othniel Marsh, in 1879 at the Morrison Formation rocks in Wyoming, USA.

COULD THIS BE TRUE?

Recent studies in the USA have concluded that foxes may well have a special sense and use Earth's magnetic fields to judge distance and direction – could *Coelurus* have had this sense as well?

FACT BOX

Palaeontologists believe that *Coelurus* may have hunted like a small modern-day predator, such as a weasel. A weasel hunts mainly by scent and, although small, it investigates every small hole and crevice it comes across until it can find its prey, then kills it with a short, sharp bite to the neck.

BONE WARS: OTHNIEL CHARLES MARSH (1831-1899)

Othniel Marsh was a famous American dinosaur hunter and is responsible for the discovery of many of the dinosaurs we know today. For example:

Allosaurus (1877), *Ammosaurus* (1890), *Anchisaurus* (1885), *Apatosaurus* (1877), *Atlantosaurus* (1877), *Barosaurus* (1890), *Camptosaurus* (1885), *Ceratops* (1888), *Ceratosaurus* (1884), *Claosaurus* (1890), *Coelurus* (1879), *Creosaurus* (1878), *Diplodocus* (1878), *Diracodon* (1881), *Dryosaurus* (1894), *Dryptosaurus* (1877), *Labrosaurus* (1896), *Laosaurus* (1878), *Nanosaurus* (1877), *Nodosaurus* (1889), *Ornithomimus* (1890), *Pleurocoelus* (1891), *Priconodon* (1888), *Stegosaurus* (1877), *Torosaurus* (1891), *Triceratops* (1889)

Marsh also competed against a fellow palaeontologist called Edward Cope in the "Bone Wars". They were both very competitive and between them discovered over 120 new species of dinosaur. Marsh triumphed in the "Bone Wars" by discovering 80 new species compared with Cope's meagre 56. Cope did not like this and they continued arguing for many years to come.

COELURUS STATS

NAME:	*Coelurus*
PRONOUNCIATION:	see-LURE-us
HEIGHT:	2.3-2.8 m (7.6-9 ft)
LENGTH:	2 m (6 ft)
DIET:	Frogs, lizards, large insects.
FOUND:	Central and Western USA
PERIOD:	Jurassic Period
DESCRIPTION:	Small bipedal carnivore with a flexible neck.

VELOCIRAPTOR

Velociraptor is one of the most infamous dinosaurs that lived during the late Cretaceous Period, around 75 million years ago. *Velociraptor* means 'speedy thief' and it would have hunted in a desert-like environment around what is now modern-day China, Mongolia and central Russia.

BEWARE OF THE BIRDS!

Some scientists believe that *Velociraptor* was very closely related to birds and may have been slightly warm-blooded, with a covering of feathers. Scientists also believe that it may have been able to breathe in a similar way to birds and keep pockets of air in its hollow bones. This would enable very fast acceleration and high speeds of up to 60 kph (37 mph).

VELOCIRAPTOR STATS

NAME:	*Velociraptor*
PRONUNCIATION:	vuh-loss-ih-RAP-tuh
HEIGHT:	80 cm (31.5 in)
LENGTH:	1.8 m (6 ft)
DIET:	Small mammals, lizards and dinosaurs.
SPEED:	60 kph (37 mph)
LIVED:	75–71 million years ago
PERIOD:	Late Cretaceous Period
FEATURES:	Hair-like filaments, large, retractable claw with three long fingers.

WHO'S A CLEVER DINO?

In comparison to its body size, *Velociraptor* had an enormous brain for a dinosaur. This probably meant it was very clever and could solve problems. It also meant that it probably hunted in packs to great effect.

MOVIE STAR

The *Velociraptor* featured in the dinosaur movie *Jurassic Park*, but it was shown to be a lot larger than palaeontologists believe.

EORAPTOR

Eoraptor is one of the earliest known dinosaurs and lived 228 million years ago during the late Triassic Period. Its fossils have been found in the foothills of the Andes in South America and its name means 'dawn plunderer'.

GREEDY DINO

Eoraptor was probably an omnivore, which means it would have eaten plants and vegetation, as well as other small reptiles and herbivorous dinosaurs.

IT'S A SMALL ONE!

Eoraptor was no taller than an average child.

SMELLY BREATH

Just like the modern-day reptile the Komodo dragon, *Eoraptor* probably had very smelly breath and teeth covered in nasty bacteria. Its front teeth were leaf-shaped, meaning it would have needed to eat soft, decaying food, such as the rotting carcasses of dead dinosaurs.

EORAPTOR STATS

NAME:	*Eoraptor*
PRONUNCIATION:	ee–oh–RAP–tor
HEIGHT:	60 cm (23.6 in)
LENGTH:	1 m (3.2 ft)
DIET:	Plants, lizards, small mammals.
LIVED:	228 million years ago
SPECIAL FEATURES:	Light, agile body with long legs and a hollow tail bone.

DID YOU KNOW?

Eoraptor had arms that were only half the length of its legs. It had sharp claws on each hand that would have been used to catch and tear its prey.

OVIRAPTOR PHILOCERATOPS

The first *Oviraptor philoceratops* fossils were discovered in the Gobi desert, Mongolia, in 1914. This strange-looking, bird-like dinosaur lived in the late Cretaceous Period, around 75 million years ago.

Fossilized dinosaur egg

OMNIVORE

Omnivore dinosaurs are quite rare as most were either carnivores (meat-eating) or herbivores (plant-eating). Omnivores will eat anything they can find and *Oviraptor philoceratops'* funny-shaped beak jaw was well equipped to deal with a variety of food, including shellfish, scavenged meat, insects, eggs and plants.

SPEEDY-SAURUS

Oviraptor philoceratops could run up to 70 kmh (43 mph).

CAUGHT RED-HANDED

Oviraptor philoceratops was thought to be an egg-stealing dinosaur, because the first fossilized skull of this dinosaur was found 10 cm (4 in) away from an egg believed to be that of a *Ceratops*. *Oviraptor* means 'egg thief' and *philoceratops* means 'like *Ceratops*'. However, a later discovery showed that the egg was that of *Oviraptor philoceratops* and that it was probably tending to its eggs rather than trying to eat them.

WOW

Scientists now believe that not all dinosaur feathers were for flight or for keeping warm. Two 125 million year old fossils found in China in 2009 show early feather formations that were for neither purpose and previously unknown to science.

DINO STATS

NAME:	*Oviraptor philoceratops*
PRONUNCIATION:	o-vih-RAP-tor
HEIGHT:	1–1.5 m (3.5 ft)
LENGTH:	1.8 m (6 ft)
DIET:	Small animals, dinosaur eggs.
LIVED:	88–70 million years ago
PERIOD:	Late Cretaceous
FEATURES:	Extremely powerful jaws and a domed crest on its head.

55

TROODON

Troodon was one of the first ever dinosaurs discovered in North America and was found in 1855. *Troodon* means 'wounding tooth', named after the serrated tooth that was the first part of the skeleton to be found. It lived all over what is modern-day western USA and Canada during the late Cretaceous period.

NEST SWEET NEST

Like the *Oviraptor philoceratops* and ground-dwelling birds, *Troodon* would make a nest on the ground and sit over its eggs like a hen.

FUSSY EATER?

Troodon's teeth were not like the teeth of typical meat-eaters. It had little serrations running up and down the back of its teeth, like most meat-eating dinosaurs did, but also larger bumps along the side like plant-eating dinosaurs. This has led some to believe that *Troodon* was not a fussy eater and may have eaten insects, eggs and even plants, as well as small animals, lizards and baby dinosaurs. This would make *Troodon* one of the rare omnivore dinosaurs.

THUMBS UP FOR INTELLIGENCE

Scientists believe that having opposable thumbs (thumbs that are in opposition to the fingers and can touch each of the fingers) has been a critical factor in human evolution. *Troodon* had opposable thumbs and a large brain (in comparison to body size). This means that, as one of the cleverest dinosaurs, it may have evolved into an even more intelligent animal, had it not become extinct.

NIGHT STALKER

Troodon had large, slightly forward-facing eyes that gave it incredible eyesight and a good sense of distance. It would have used these eyes to its advantage when hunting at dusk or twilight.

ROBO-SAURUS

Scientists at MIT in Cambridge, USA, have built 'Troody', a robotic version of *Troodon*, to see how the 3.5 m (12 ft) long and 1 m (3 ft) tall dinosaur would have walked and kept its balance.

57

ACROCANTHOSAURUS

Acrocanthosaurus means 'high-spined lizard'. It lived in the early Cretaceous Period, roughly 115–105 million years ago and its habitat was in the tropics, near sea level. Its name came from the unusual spikes that grew on its spine. 'Acro', as the dinosaur is often nicknamed, was 13 m (42 ft) long and weighed 2300 kg (5000 lbs). It was a meat-eater and was a large, fierce predator that could kill even large sauropods. *Acrocanthosaurus* is thought to have been a scavenger, too. Its teeth were designed for tearing meat from the bones of its prey.

STRONGER THAN YOU THINK!

This dinosaur would probably be able to lift a small car off the ground if it were alive today. Its arms were larger and more powerful than those of *Tyrannosaurus rex.*

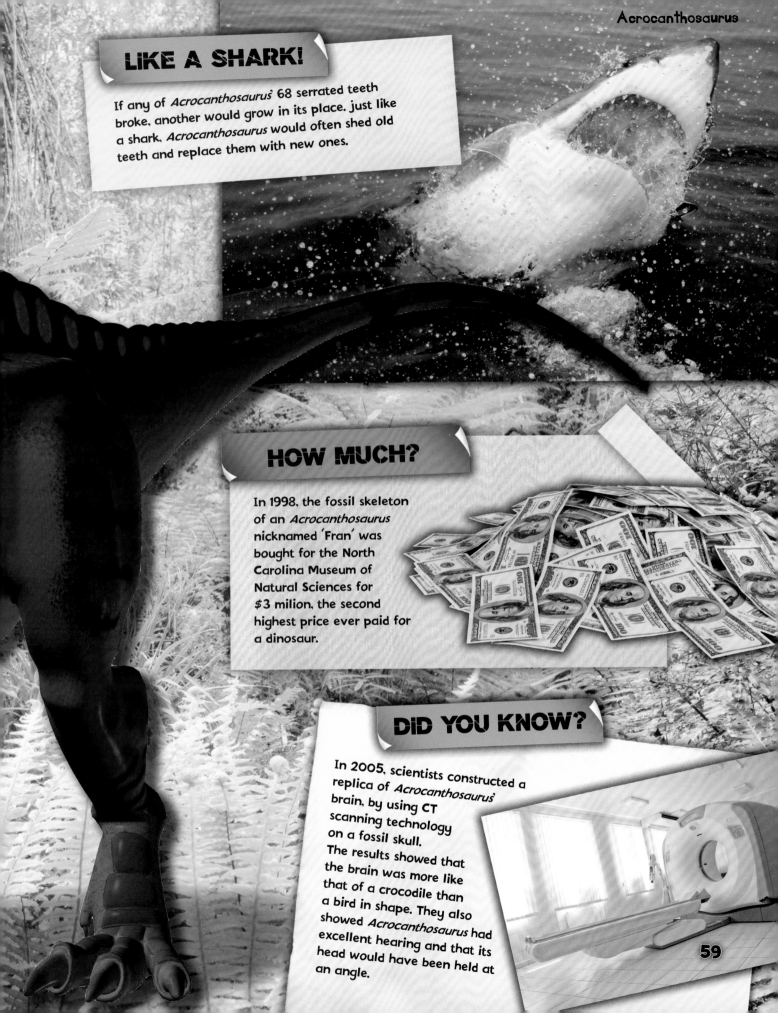

LIKE A SHARK!

If any of *Acrocanthosaurus'* 68 serrated teeth broke, another would grow in its place. Just like a shark, *Acrocanthosaurus* would often shed old teeth and replace them with new ones.

HOW MUCH?

In 1998, the fossil skeleton of an *Acrocanthosaurus* nicknamed 'Fran' was bought for the North Carolina Museum of Natural Sciences for $3 milion, the second highest price ever paid for a dinosaur.

DID YOU KNOW?

In 2005, scientists constructed a replica of *Acrocanthosaurus'* brain, by using CT scanning technology on a fossil skull. The results showed that the brain was more like that of a crocodile than a bird in shape. They also showed *Acrocanthosaurus* had excellent hearing and that its head would have been held at an angle.

MEGALOSAURUS

Megalosaurus means 'great lizard'. It is thought to have lived in the forests of what is now Western Europe, during the late Jurassic Period, around 160 million years ago. This carnivore grew to a length of 9 m (30 ft) and weighed about a ton. It walked on two legs and had a long tail to help it balance. *Megalosaurus* was a powerful hunter and could attack large prey. It probably also scavenged meat from dead bodies as part of its diet. Its back legs were much longer than its arms and it had hands that might have been used for grasping. *Megalosaurus* was the first of the ancient dinosaurs to be named and described by scientists.

Fossils have been found in Europe, Asia, Africa and South America.

A GIANT MAN?

Megalosaurus was named in 1826 and was the first dinosaur to be given a name. In 1676 a fossilized femur of *Megalosaurus* was dug up in England and was thought to belong to a giant man! It was 150 years later that the dinosaur was named by palaeontologist William Buckland.

WALKED LIKE A DUCK

Scientists have studied *Megalosaurus'* fossilized footprints, which show that its feet pointed inwards as it walked. The dinosaur probably would have waddled like a duck, with its tail swishing from side to side!

DINO STATS

NAME:	*Megalosaurus*
PRONUNCIATION:	MEG-uh-lo-SAWR-us
HEIGHT:	3 m (10 ft)
LENGTH:	9 m (30 ft)
DIET:	Other dinosaurs
PERIOD:	Middle Jurassic Period
LIVED:	166 million years ago
FEATURES:	Curved teeth.

DID YOU KNOW?

Scientists have estimated that *Megalosaurus* could run at around 29 kph (18 mph), although it would have usually plodded along at around 7 kph (4 mph).

SPINOSAURUS

Spinosaurus means 'spined lizard'. This dinosaur is named after the row of high spines running down its backbone. These probably had skin stretched between them to form a 'sail' up to 2 m (6 ft) tall. This enormous dinosaur lived in the late Cretaceous Period, around 98–95 million years ago, in what we now know as Africa. *Spinosaurus* walked on two legs and had a long, slender nose with jaws resembling a crocodile. Its teeth were not sharp or made for ripping flesh like *Giganotosaurus*, but were long, cone-shaped and interlocked. This suggests that its main diet was probably fish.

MOVIE STAR

Spinosaurus is the main villain of the movie, *Jurassic Park III.* In the movie, *Spinosaurus* battles with *Tyrannosaurus rex* and eventually comes out the winner.

BIG HEAD!

Spinosaurus had a skull that was 1.75 m (5 ft 9 in). That's as long as an average man!

WOW, MASSIVE!

In February 2006, it was revealed that *Spinosaurus* was the biggest meat-eating dinosaur of all, even bigger than *Tyrannosaurus rex.* It measured 17 m (56 ft) long and would have weighed 7–9 tons.

FOSSIL FACTS

The first *Spinosaurus* fossils were discovered in Egypt in 1911, by the German geologist and palaeontologist Ernst Stromer.

CARNOTAURUS

Carnotaurus means 'meat-eating bull'. It was another enormous dinosaur that lived during the Cretaceous Period, around 113–91 million years ago, in what is now Argentina. It had a small skull, a broad chest and a thin tail, as well as unusually small arms. *Carnotaurus* was bipedal and grew to about 7.6 m (25 ft) long and stood about 4.6 m (15 ft) high. We do not know if it had the speed and agility to hunt down prey, but its short, pointed teeth show us it was a meat-eater. Instead of hunting, it may have scavenged from the bodies of dead animals.

HORNS OF A BULL

Carnotaurus was named in 1985 by José F Bonaparte, after its most notable feature – the two bull-like horns located above its eyes. The first and only *Carnotaurus* fossil was found by Bonaparte in Patagonia, South America.

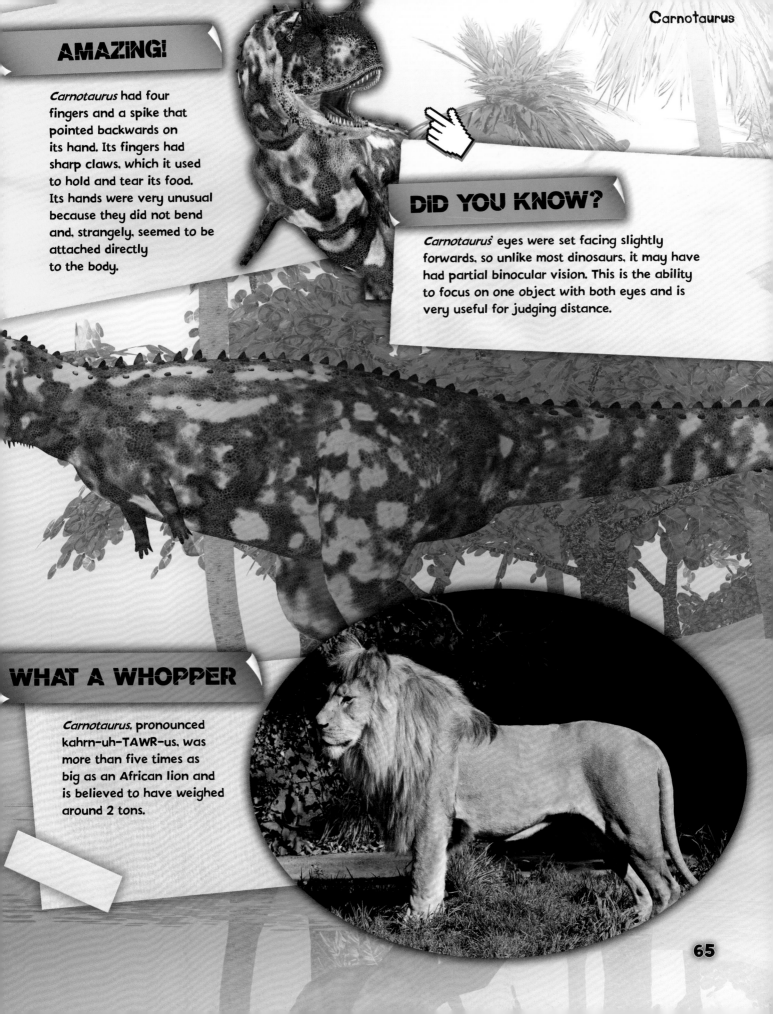

AMAZING!

Carnotaurus had four fingers and a spike that pointed backwards on its hand. Its fingers had sharp claws, which it used to hold and tear its food. Its hands were very unusual because they did not bend and, strangely, seemed to be attached directly to the body.

DID YOU KNOW?

Carnotaurus' eyes were set facing slightly forwards, so unlike most dinosaurs, it may have had partial binocular vision. This is the ability to focus on one object with both eyes and is very useful for judging distance.

WHAT A WHOPPER

Carnotaurus, pronounced kahrn-uh-TAWR-us, was more than five times as big as an African lion and is believed to have weighed around 2 tons.

SAURORNITHOIDES

Saurornithoides means 'bird-like lizard'. This dinosaur was a highly efficient predator that roamed the plains of what is now Central Asia, during the Cretaceous Period, around 70-65 million years ago. It had a long, low head and sharp, closely packed teeth. It was between 2-3 m (6-10 ft) in length and weighed about 13-27 kg (29-59 lbs). Like other raptors, it ran on its strong hind legs and probably used its grasping hands to seize and tear at live prey. It ate small mammals and possibly other dinosaur hatchlings.

AWESOME EYES

Saurornithoides would have been sharp-eyed, as it had large eyes and binocular vision. It also would have had excellent night vision. Some scientists believe it may have been primarily nocturnal when hunting for prey.

DID YOU KNOW?

Saurornithoides had an especially long, vicious claw on its hind feet, which was attached to the fourth toe and was retractable when running or walking.

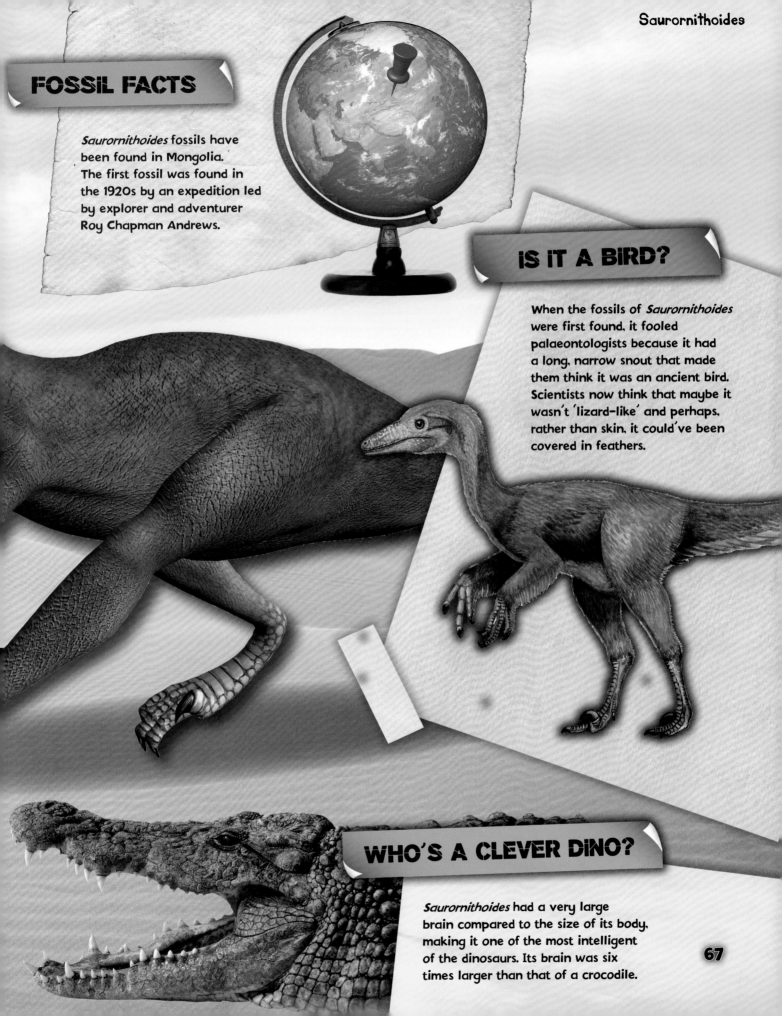

FOSSIL FACTS

Saurornithoides fossils have been found in Mongolia. The first fossil was found in the 1920s by an expedition led by explorer and adventurer Roy Chapman Andrews.

IS IT A BIRD?

When the fossils of *Saurornithoides* were first found, it fooled palaeontologists because it had a long, narrow snout that made them think it was an ancient bird. Scientists now think that maybe it wasn't 'lizard-like' and perhaps, rather than skin, it could've been covered in feathers.

WHO'S A CLEVER DINO?

Saurornithoides had a very large brain compared to the size of its body, making it one of the most intelligent of the dinosaurs. Its brain was six times larger than that of a crocodile.

67

COLOUR AND CAMOUFLAGE

Nobody knows for sure what colour dinosaurs actually were, although they are often shown as green or brown. There is no way to know, because an animal's skin colour is produced by organic pigments that are not preserved when fossils are formed. Scientists do know, however, that dinosaurs were covered with tough, scaly skin, like modern reptiles. While large meat-eaters and armoured dinosaurs may not have needed camouflage, the smaller ones would have needed this kind of defence to hide from predators.

DINO DATING

It is likely that dinosaurs would have used colour as a method to attract a mate, similar to modern-day animals. Colour can announce that a male is ready to breed and helps females choose a mate.

RED ARMOUR

Stegosaurus had two rows of diamond-shaped plates along its back and each of these plates were filled with tiny blood vessels. If *Stegosaurus* needed to cool down, blood would be pumped into these plates, which would have turned them bright red.

SCAN ME
Instructions on page 5

DID YOU KNOW?

Bright colours in nature normally mean that an animal, or plant is a member of a poisonous species.

CAMOUFLAGE FACT

Like animals today, dinosaurs probably used colour to conceal, disguise and identify themselves. Dinosaurs more than likely had pale undersides to reduce shadows and striped or spotted patterns to help them blend in among plants and vegetation.

STRIPY SKIN

A recent discovery of a mummified *Hadrosaur* provided scientists with a fossilized sample of its skin, which indicated that the animal may have had stripes along its tail.

BLENDING IN

Camouflage is important for many animals and insects in our world. It is difficult for scientists to know exactly how dinosaurs camouflaged themselves within their environment, as fossils provide them with little evidence on this. However, by looking at modern-day animals and insects, we can speculate on how dinosaurs may have been patterned and coloured.

BRACHIOSAURUS

Brachiosaurus was once thought to be the biggest dinosaur ever discovered. Its name means 'arm lizard', because its front legs were longer than its back legs. *Brachiosaurus* was discovered in 1900 and fossils have been found in both the USA and Africa. It probably moved around in large family herds (like elephants) and it lived during the late Jurassic Period. It was a herbivore and would have eaten ferns, bushes and grazed the tree-tops with its long neck.

IT'S HUGE!

Look how this *Brachiosaurus* compares with a man standing underneath. It was massive, weighing a whopping 77 tons (20 times that of a large elephant), measuring 25 m (82 ft) long and standing tall at 15 m (49 ft) high.

GREEDY DINO

The *Brachiosaurus* had to eat about 200 kg (440 lbs) of food every day just to fuel its massive body. So they could digest all this food, these dinosaurs also swallowed stones which helped grind down the tough leaves and plant fibres.

DID YOU KNOW?

Each *Brachiosaurus* may have lived to be over 100 years old.

COME AND SEE ME

If you visit Chicago O'Hare International Airport in the U.S.A, you can see a full-sized *Brachiosaurus*. It is 23 m (75 ft) long and 12 m (40 ft) high. This is an exact replica made out of fibreglass of a fossil that was unearthed in the Grand Junction, Colorado in 1900.

HERD INSTINCT

Brachiosaurus probably travelled in herds This wasn't because they were sociable creatures, but because by travelling with lots of others they were less likely to be attacked and more likely to receive help if they were.

GENTLE GIANT WITH A BIG HEART

So that blood could be pumped all the way up its long neck, *Brachiosaurus* needed a very large and muscular heart. Owing to the difficulty of pumping blood around such a large body, some scientists believe that *Brachiosaurus* must have been warm-blooded, while others believe the neck was always kept parallel to the floor.

ARGENTINOSAURUS

If *Brachiosaurus* was large, *Argentinosaurus* was massive!
It is believed to be the biggest land-dwelling animal ever, growing to even greater lengths than the blue whale. It lived during the late Cretaceous Period.

WOW, AMAZING!

Owing to its long neck, the *Argentinosaurus* would have easily been able to peer in through a fourth storey window of a skyscraper!

ARGENTINOSAURUS FACT FILE

Height: 21.4 m (70 ft)
Length: 36.5 m (120 ft)
Diet: Tough plant material
Lived: 97–94 million years ago
Period: Late Cretaceous Period

ARGENTINA – THE LAND OF THE GIANTS

Some of the worlds largest dinosaurs have been found in South America, in particular Argentina. The largest meat-eating dinosaur, the scary *Giganotosaurus*, lived at the same time as the largest ever dinosaur, *Argentinosaurus*. *Giganotosaurus* may have hunted in packs and it may have hunted the *Argentinosaurus*, which would have been a truly gigantic fight.

DID YOU KNOW?

Argentinosaurus was as long as four buses!

A LOT OF MESS!

Just like the *Brachiosaurus*, *Argentinosaurus* had to eat a massive amount to fuel its gigantic body. It would have spent most of its life eating. At this time in Patagonia, Argentina, finding food would not have been hard. It was a lush land, full of conifers, seeds, fruits and flowering plants. Scientists have estimated that the *Argentinosaurus* would have passed at least 15 l (3 gal) of dung a day!

73

DIPLODOCUS

The name *Diplodocus* means 'double-beamed lizard'. This comes from the fact that the bones in the middle of its tail run both backwards and forwards. *Diplodocus* is a quadruped and it lived in what is now western North America, in the late Jurassic Period. Although it was massive and scary in size, *Diplodocus* was a herbivore and is thought to have spent virtually all day long eating leaves and foliage, such as ferns. However, *Diplodocus* couldn't chew, so it swallowed small stones to help grind up the food inside its stomach.

DID YOU KNOW?

The only fossils of *Diplodocus* to have been found so far are in North America in Colorado, Montana, Utah and Wyoming. This is not to say that they didn't live anywhere else, but based on what has been found, *Diplodocus* was a true American!

SAY IT PROPERLY

Diplodocus is pronounced **DIP-low-DOE-kuss.**

FACTS CHANGE WITH TIME

Early research suggested that Diplodocus might have swum in water, but more recent studies have indicated that the massive water pressure on its chest would have made it difficult for Diplodocus to breathe. It used to be thought that sauropods had a second brain. Palaeontologists now think that what they thought was a second brain was simply a large spinal cord in the hip area.

DIPLODOCUS STATS

Height: 6 m (20 ft)
Length: 27 m (89 ft)
Lived: 155–146 million years ago
Features: Long neck, whiplash tail,
                  hollow bones, tiny head.

AWESOME FACT

Diplodocus was one of the longest animals ever to have lived on planet Earth!

FAST TAIL

Some palaeontologists believe that Diplodocus used its tail as a weapon. However, owing to its massive size, physicists have shown that, if that were the case, the speed achieved at the very tip of the tail would have broken the sound barrier!

APATOSAURUS

Apatosaurus is another giant herbivore that grazed the plains during the Jurassic Period, 150 million years ago. Its name means 'deceptive lizard', because of its resemblance to a group of prehistoric marine lizards. Just like *Diplodocus*, *Apatosaurus* had peg-like teeth, ideal for stripping leaves. As it would have eaten almost constantly when awake, to fuel its massive body, it was lucky to have nostrils on top of its skull, so that it could eat and breathe at the same time.

MMMM, TASTY!

Big dinosaurs, such as *Apatosaurus*, would have swallowed stones to help with digestion by grinding up tough leaves and fibrous plants.
These stones were called 'gastroliths'.

THE DINOSAUR FORMERLY KNOWN AS 'BRONTOSAURUS'

QUICK FACTS:

Height: 3–4.6 m (10–15 ft)
Length: 21–27 m (69–90 ft)
Diet: Tough plant material

Apatosaurus means 'deceptive lizard' and was found and named by the famous palaeontologist, Othniel Marsh, in 1877. In 1879, he found and named a new dinosaur called *Brontosaurus*. However, in 1903, it was discovered that *Brontosaurus* was just a fully grown *Apatosaurus*. Despite this, the name *Brontosaurus* is still popular and was not removed from the official naming list until 1974.

THE MAN-EATING HERBIVORE

In the 1933 movie *King Kong*, *Apatosaurus* was portrayed as a blood-thirsty carnivore, not as the gentle plant-eating dinosaur we know it to be.

A BIG WALKING JUICY PIECE OF STEAK

Or so *Allosaurus*, which hunted *Apatosaurus*, thought. *Allosaurus* tooth marks have been found in the fossilized vertebrae of *Apatosaurus*. However, *Apatosaurus* had a trick up its sleeve for protection. It was so large that when it lifted its head, *Allosaurus* would not have been able to reach its head or neck, the most vulnerable parts of its body.

BIG FOOT

Forget the mysterious Big Foot! Some *Apatosaurus* footprints discovered have been measured at 1 m (3 ft) across!

EGGS AWAY!

Some scientists believe that because these giant dinosaurs and their eggs were so large, they simply laid the eggs as they walked along and did not need to look after them.

77

SEISMOSAURUS

Known as 'earthquake lizard', *Seismosaurus* was named because its massive size would have shaken the ground with every step it took. It was discovered in 1979, but because of its gigantic size and the large rocks where the fossil was found, it took 13 years for archaeologists to excavate it. The skeleton is still not complete today!

WOW, REALLY?

Seismosaurus probably hatched from eggs like other sauropods. They are also thought to have lived to over 100 years old, giving them a very long lifespan compared to other dinosaurs.

STOMACH OF STONE

In 1979, the fossilized bones of a *Seismosaurus* were discovered in New Mexico, USA. Palaeontologists also found more than 200 gastroliths in its stomach, which are small stones that *Seismosaurus* would have swallowed to help digestion.

WHAT A TRAGIC END!

One *Seismosaurus* fossil specimen found is believed to have tragically died by swallowing a stone that was too large and so lodged in its throat and blocked its ability to breathe.

DID YOU KNOW?

Seismosaurus' long neck would have usually been held parallel to the ground. It might have allowed the creature to poke its head into dense forest areas to reach leaves otherwise inaccessible to bulky dinosaurs, or maybe to eat soft pteridophytes that grew in wet areas too swampy to enter safely.

MEGA STATS

Seismosaurus is at the top of the 'longest dinosaur' list.

It was 35 m (115 ft) long and weighed 22000 kg (50000 lbs).

HADROSAURUS

Although this dinosaur could arguably be said to resemble a much larger version of our modern-day horse, the name *Hadrosaurus* actually means 'heavy lizard'. In 1838, *Hadrosaurus* was unintentionally discovered in Haddonfield, New Jersey. It was initially uncovered by John Hopkins, who found giant bones in a claypit, but thought nothing of them and took them home and put them in a cabinet. Some 20 years later, a visitor named William Foulke spotted the bones and went to the pit to explore further. Foulke then contacted a palaeontologist and together they recovered the fossils and named the dinosaur *Hadrosaurus*.

DID YOU KNOW?

Hadrosaurus was the first almost complete dinosaur to be discovered. It was also the first ever dinosaur fossil to be mounted and put on display in a museum.

HE WAS RIGHT!

In 1841, long before *Hadrosaurus*'s naming, a British man named Dr Richard Owen suggested that these large bones probably belonged to a group of large reptiles that had become extinct from Earth. He called them 'Dinosaurs', meaning 'terrible lizards'. However, at the time, no one believed him.

HOW DO YOU SAY MY NAME

HAD-ruh-SAWR-us

BRONZE DINO

In October 2003, a bronze statue of *Hadrosaurus* was completed in the state of New Jersey. This statue was created to the same size as *Hadrosaurus* would have been. It was unveiled in Haddonfield, near to where the first fossil was found.

MELANOROSAURUS

Melanorosaurus means 'black mountain lizard' and it lived in the early Triassic Period, around 225–205 million years ago, in what is now the woodlands of South Africa. *Melanorosaurus* was a plant-eater and had a bulky body, long neck and a relatively small skull and brain. Its erect limbs would have been similar to the limbs of an elephant. Its diet would have consisted of branches, leaves and twigs, which, given its height and long neck, would have been easy to reach the tops of trees. Serrated, leaf-shaped teeth would have allowed it to snap off branches and then chew the vegetation quite effectively before swallowing.

LARGEST OF ITS TIME!

Melanorosaurus was the biggest dinosaur of the Triassic Period. At 12 m (39 ft) long and weighing around 2250 kg (5000 lbs), it was the largest dinosaur of its day. It was only in the Jurassic Period and later that larger dinosaurs have been found.

DID YOU KNOW?

Melanorosaurus would have had the ability to walk on two legs, but it didn't have to. This is called a 'facultative biped'. It may have taken advantage of this skill to reach high up, tasty leaves!

BONE FACT

While *Melanorosaurus'* limbs had dense bones, its spinal bones and vertebrae were hollow to reduce their weight.

FOSSIL FACT

Melanorosaurus (pronounced MEH-lan-OH-roe-SAW-rus) was named by the British palaeontologist Sydney H. Haugh in 1924.

It was named after the Thaba Nyama or 'black mountain' in South Africa where the fossil was found.

83

SALTASAURUS

Saltasaurus, a herbivore, belonged to the sauropod group, which meant that it had a long neck, small head and long tail. However, fossil discoveries have shown that *Saltasaurus* was smaller than most other sauropods. *Saltasaurus* means 'lizard from Salta' and it lived during the Cretaceous Period. It would have grown to around 12 m (39 ft) long and weighed approximately 8 tons.

COOL!

The name *Saltasaurus* means 'lizard from Salta'. The first *Saltasaurus* was discovered in Salta, Argentina in 1980, by José Bonaparte and Jaime Powell.

DEFENSIVE ARMOUR PLATING

Saltasaurus is currently the only discovered sauropod that had armour plating. Both its back and sides were covered in circular and oval bony plates up to 12 cm (5 in) in diameter. It is also possible that horns or spikes may have stuck out for extra defence. It is likely that the armour and any spikes were slowly introduced to the *Saltasaurus* as a result of evolution. Owing to its inferior size compared to other large plant-eaters, *Saltasaurus* has now been reclassified as an ankylosaur.

DID YOU KNOW?

Communal nest-building shows that *Saltasaurus* probably lived and travelled in herds.

HOW DO YOU SAY MY NAME?

salt-uh-SAWR-us

85

CAMARASAURUS

Camarasaurus means 'chambered lizard' and it lived during the late Jurassic Period, around 155–145 million years ago. *Camarasaurus* looked a bit like *Diplodocus,* with a long neck and tail. It was a large herbivore and although it wasn't as big as other sauropods, it still weighed up to 20 tons!

CAMARASAURUS STATS:

PRONUNICATION: kuh–MARE–uh–SAWR–us
HEIGHT: 7 m (23 ft)
LENGTH: 15–23 m (50–75 ft)
DIET: Wide variety
                 of plants.

DID YOU KNOW?

The name 'chambered lizard' comes from the holes in the vertebrae that decreased its weight.

CAMARASAURUS FOSSILS

Camarasaurus fossils have been found in Colorado, New Mexico, Utah, and Wyoming. *Camarasaurus* was named in 1877 by Edward Cope.

SUPERSAURUS

Supersaurus, meaning 'super lizard', was a sauropod that lived around 153 million years ago. It is one of the largest dinosaurs ever found and is thought to have reached up to 34 m (112 ft) in length. *Supersaurus* should not be confused with *Ultrasaurus*, a much smaller dinosaur discovered in South Korea. *Ultrasaurus* in turn has a similar name to *Ultrasauros*, another type of *Supersaurus*, once thought to be a separate, giant sauropod.

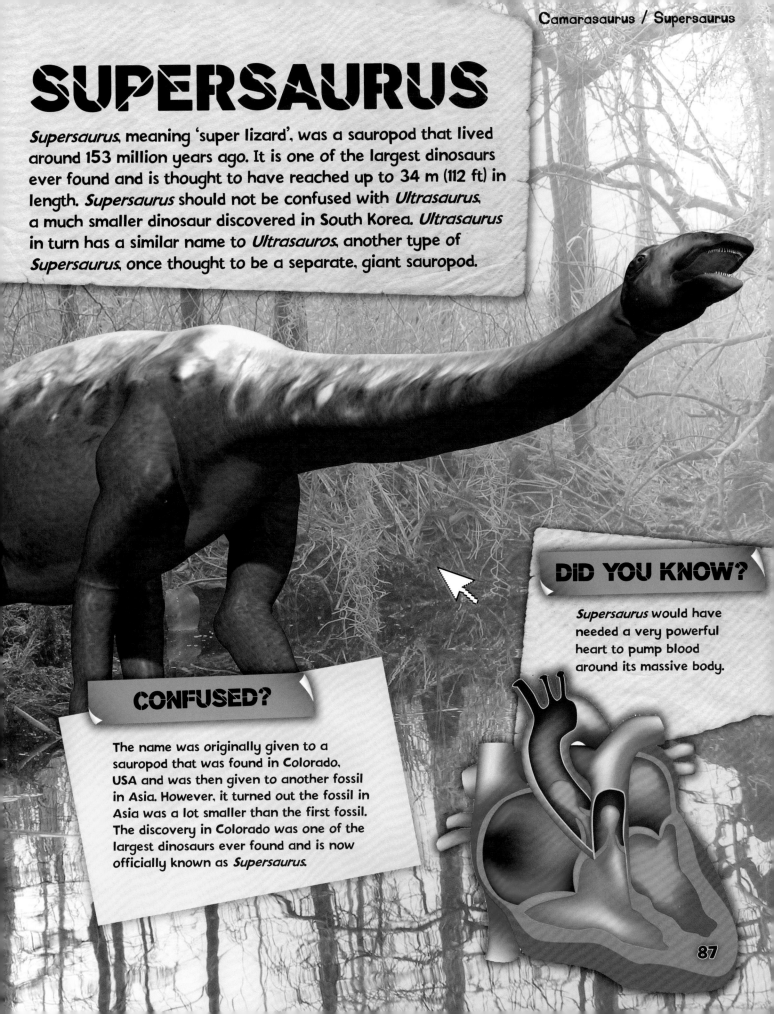

DID YOU KNOW?

Supersaurus would have needed a very powerful heart to pump blood around its massive body.

CONFUSED?

The name was originally given to a sauropod that was found in Colorado, USA and was then given to another fossil in Asia. However, it turned out the fossil in Asia was a lot smaller than the first fossil. The discovery in Colorado was one of the largest dinosaurs ever found and is now officially known as *Supersaurus*.

COLD-BLOODED CREATURES

People disagree over whether dinosaurs were cold-blooded or warm-blooded. It was once believed that dinosaurs were cold-blooded like their reptile ancestors. Palaeontologists have recently argued that at least some of the dinosaurs were fast, active and that they competed against warm-blooded mammals. Since some dinosaurs lived in cool areas and were related to birds, scientists think they might have been warm-blooded.

WARM-BLOODED CREATURES?

Warm-blooded creatures include humans, mammals and birds. They regulate the temperature inside their bodies to a constant temperature. They generate heat when they are in a cooler environment and cool themselves when they are in a hotter environment.
To generate heat, warm-blooded animals convert the food they eat into energy.
They eat a lot of food compared with their cold-blooded relations and most of this food is used to fuel a constant body temperature.

FACT FOR THE WARM-BLOODED CASE

Many of the big dinosaurs, such as *Tyrannosaurus rex* and *Iguanodon*, held their heads high above their bodies. To do this they would have needed two blood circuits and an internally divided heart, which would make them warm-blooded.

COLD-BLOODED CREATURES

Cold-blooded creatures include reptiles, insects, arachnids, amphibians and fish. They take on the temperature of their surroundings. For example, when the environment is hot, they are hot and when the environment is cold, they are cold. Cold-blooded animals are much slower in cold environments. Their muscle activity is dependent on chemical reactions that function much more quickly in hotter temperatures. They are often found sunning themselves in the morning to warm up and get going.

FACT FOR THE COLD-BLOODED CASE

Dinosaurs like *Spinosaurus* and *Ouranosaurus* had large sails on their backs, which were probably used for collection and removal of heat. This suggests they were cold-blooded.

DID YOU KNOW?

In 2000, the fossil of a *Thescelosaurus* was found to have a mammal-like four-chambered heart, suggesting it was warm-blooded.

ICHTHYOSAURUS

Ichthyosaurus was an ichthyosaur and its name meant 'fish lizard'. It lived from the early Jurassic Period until the early Cretaceous Period, roughly 206–140 million years ago. *Ichthyosaurus* was a marine reptile, not a dinosaur. *Ichthyosaurus* looked a bit like a bluefin tuna, and the first complete fossil was found in England.

WOW, SPEEDY!

Ichthyosaurus was about 2 m (6.5 ft) long and would have weighed about 90 kg (200 lbs). This sleek animal may have swum at speeds up to 40 kph (25 mph).

DID YOU KNOW?

Hundreds of *Ichthyosaurus* fossils have been found in England, Germany, Greenland and Canada.

HOW DO YOU SAY MY NAME?

ICK-the-oh-SAWR-us

AWESOME HEARING!

One odd feature of *Ichthyosaurus* is that it possessed thick, massive ear bones, which might have conveyed subtle vibrations in the surrounding water to this reptile's inner ear. This may have helped it catching food.

IMPORTANT FAMILY!

You may have guessed from its name, *Ichthyosaurus* has lent its name to an important family of marine reptiles, the ichthyosaurs, which descended from terrestrial reptiles that ventured into the water during the late Triassic Period. In the late Jurassic Period, the ichthyosaurs produced some really massive relatives, most notably the 9 m (30 ft) long *Shonisaurus*.

91

ELASMOSAURUS

Elasmosaurus, meaning 'ribbon lizard', was a long-necked marine reptile that was up to 14 m (46 ft) long. It lived in the late Cretaceous Period, around 70 million years ago. Half of its length was its neck, which had about 75 vertebrae. *Elasmosaurus* had four long, paddle-like flippers, a tiny head, sharp teeth in strong jaws and a pointed tail. It was the longest of the plesiosaurs.

YOU'LL NEVER GUESS WHAT!

The land mass in the late Cretaceous Period was very different from today. The first fossil of the plesiosaur *Elasmosaurus* was discovered in 1868 in landlocked Kansas — not the first place you'd think to dig up a marine reptile! 70 million years ago, much of North America was submerged beneath the Western Interior Sea and many remains of icthyosaurs, plesiosaurs and mosasaurs have been found there.

HOW DID IT EAT?

Elasmosaurus had an enormously long neck that could be 7.6 m (25 ft) long, which is 4 times longer than a giraffe's neck! This unusual feature has led to some disagreement about how *Elasmosaurus* hunted for fish. Some palaeontologists think it bent its head sideways around its body, while others believe this reptile swam on the surface and used its long neck to scope out prey.

WHICH END IS THE HEAD!

Elasmosaurus was the cause of one of the pettier disputes in 19th-century palaeontology, the Bone Wars. It began when the famous fossil-hunter, Edward Drinker Cope, mistook this plesiosaur's long neck for its tail – and placed the head on the wrong end! Cope's rival, Othniel C Marsh, took great pleasure in pointing out the error and the two palaeontologists spent the rest of the 19th century in a bitter feud.

HOW DO YOU SAY MY NAME?

e-LAS-mo-SAWR-us

KRONOSAURUS

Kronosaurus lived during the Cretaceous Period, around 110 million years ago. *Kronosaurus* was a classic example of a pliosaur, a type of marine reptile. It had an enormous head, short neck and outsized flipper. *Kronosaurus* lived in the seas that covered parts of what is now Australia.

WOW, GREEDY!

Kronosaurus appears to be much like a modern great white shark, simply eating any fish, squid and other marine reptiles that swam across its path. It was fast, fierce and one of the top predators of the prehistoric ocean. The 'Kronos' in this giant's name derives from the ancient Greek god who ate his own children in an attempt to preserve his power.

BIG BUT NOT THAT BIG!

Although *Kronosaurus* was big, it didn't approach the bulk of the most massive pliosaur of all time, *Liopleurodon*, which may have weighed as much as 35 tons compared to about 10 tons for the largest *Kronosaurus*. However, both of these reptiles were outclassed by the giant shark, Megalodon, which lived tens of millions of years later and weighed about 50 tons.

WOW, FACT!

Kronosaurus lived in the open oceans and breathed air. Some pliosaurs have been found with small stones in their stomachs. These may have been used to help grind up their food, or as extra weight to help them dive. They probably laid eggs in beach sand like modern-day sea turtles.

SCAN ME
Instructions on page 5

DID YOU KNOW?

Kronosaurus means 'Kronos lizard' (pronounced CROW-no-SORE-us). *Kronosaurus* fossils have been found in Australia and Colombia. It was discovered in Queensland, Australia, in 1889 by A. Crombie and was originally thought to be an ichthyosaur. It was named and described by Longman in 1924.

TYLOSAURUS

Tylosaurus was a large, predatory marine reptile that lived during the late Cretaceous Period, around 85–80 million years ago. *Tylosaurus* is named after its large snout, useful for hunting prey. Fossils of this mosasaur have been found in North America and New Zealand. *Tylosaurus* ate other sea creatures, such as fish, sharks and smaller mosasaurs. It even ate diving *Pteranodon* that got too close to the sea surface.

OPEN WIDE!

Tylosaurus rarely bit off more than it could chew – it was able to flex its lower jaw, allowing it to open its mouth very wide and swallow large prey in one piece, just like a modern-day snake!

HOW BIG?

Tylosaurus was a marine reptile known as a mosasaur. It was one of the biggest of the mosasaurs, growing up to 13 m (43 ft) long.

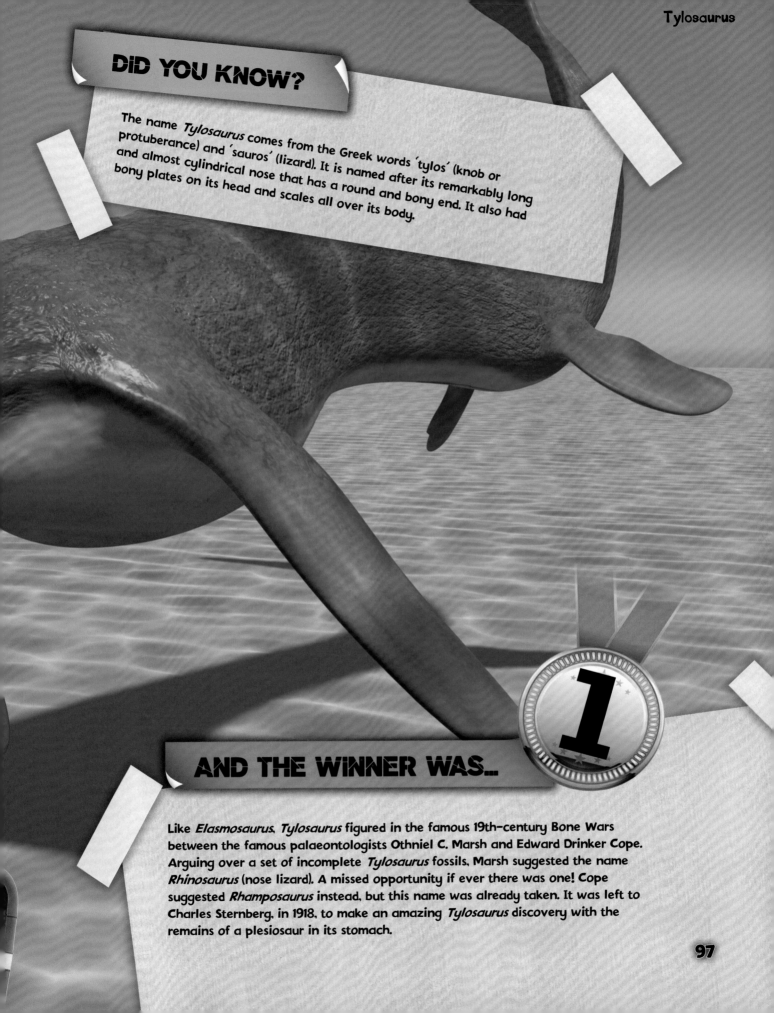

DID YOU KNOW?

The name *Tylosaurus* comes from the Greek words 'tylos' (knob or protuberance) and 'sauros' (lizard). It is named after its remarkably long and almost cylindrical nose that has a round and bony end. It also had bony plates on its head and scales all over its body.

AND THE WINNER WAS...

Like *Elasmosaurus*, *Tylosaurus* figured in the famous 19th-century Bone Wars between the famous palaeontologists Othniel C. Marsh and Edward Drinker Cope. Arguing over a set of incomplete *Tylosaurus* fossils, Marsh suggested the name *Rhinosaurus* (nose lizard). A missed opportunity if ever there was one! Cope suggested *Rhamposaurus* instead, but this name was already taken. It was left to Charles Sternberg, in 1918, to make an amazing *Tylosaurus* discovery with the remains of a plesiosaur in its stomach.

97

MOSASAURUS

The fearsome *Mosasaurus* was a giant member of the mosasaur family of marine reptiles. It had a big, alligator-like head, powerful jaws and front and rear flippers. It lived during the late Cretaceous Period, around 70–65 million years ago. It is directly related to modern-day monitor lizards and was named after the Meuse River where it was first discovered.

ONE OF THE EARLIEST!

Mosasaurus is named after the River Meuse near Maastricht in the Netherlands, where the first fossil specimen was found. It was given the name in 1822, making *Mosasaurus* one of the earliest dinosaur fossils to be discovered. These discoveries led early naturalists to identify for the first time that currently extinct species had once lived on Earth, which went against the accepted religious beliefs of the time.

FANCY A DRINK!

In 1795, a *Mosasaurus* skull was traded to the occupying French army for 600 bottles of wine! It now sits in a Paris museum.

WHAT'S FOR LUNCH?

The preserved stomach contents of *Mosasaurus* fossils show them to have eaten sharks, bony fish, turtles and other marine reptiles. *Mosasaurus* was one of the most ferocious aquatic predators of its time.

EEL MOTION

Mosasaurus had about 100 vertebrae in its back, each joined to the next by a flexible ball-and-socket joint. This would have allowed *Mosasaurus* to move in the water like an eel.

DID THEY, DIDN'T THEY!

Scientists cannot agree as to whether *Mosasaurus* came onto land to lay eggs, like turtles, or gave birth to live young in the water.

PLESIOSAURUS

Plesiosaurus was a sauropterygian which lived during the Jurassic Period, around 135–120 million years ago. It had a small head, long neck and body, a bit like a modern-day turtle. It also had four paddle-like flippers and could grow to 2.3 m (7.6 ft) long. Some people believe that the Loch Ness Monster is a modern-day plesiosaur!

DID YOU KNOW?

Plesiosaurus fossils were among some of the earliest fossil discoveries, which created a sensation back in the early 19th century as scientists didn't know quite what to make of them. It was first found by the famous fossil hunter Mary Anning in 1821 and was later named by H.T. De La Beche and William D. Conybeare. *Plesiosaurus* fossils have been found in England and Germany. In 2004, a fully intact fossilized young *Plesiosaurus* was found about 50 km (31 miles) north of where the first *Plesiosaurus* was found.

NOT THE BEST!

Plesiosaurus was probably not the most accomplished of swimmers. It lacked the hydrodynamic shapes of their bigger, meaner and more streamlined cousins, the pliosaurs.

ONE OF THE FIRST!

The first *Plesiosaurus* fossil was found long before the first dinosaur fossil.

WOW, FAMOUS!

A *Plesiosaurus* is one of the creatures mentioned in Jules Verne's *Journey to the Centre of the Earth*, where it battles with an ichthyosaur.

FISH AND STONES FOR LUNCH!

Fossilized remains found in the stomachs of *Plesiosaurus* fossils show that they ate fish and other swimming animals. We know they also swallowed small stones. It is believed that this was either to help break up their food or to help weigh them down for diving deeper into the ocean.

NOTHOSAURUS

Nothosaurus, meaning 'false reptile', was a fish-eating reptile which lived during the Triassic period, around 250-210 million years ago. *Nothosaurus* had four wide, paddle-like limbs with webbed fingers and toes. These reptiles had a long, thin head with many sharp teeth. Its nostrils were on the top end of the snout. It could reach up to 4 m (13 ft) long. Some think that it evolved into a plesiosaur and fossils have been discovered in North Africa, China and Europe. *Nothosaurus* did not live in water all the time. It would have come up onto rocks and beaches to rest, just like a seal. Although it was a good swimmer, it wasn't well adapted to living in the water full-time. *Nothosaurus* was even featured in Disney's *Fantasia*!

DIET

Nothosaurus liked to eat fish and shrimp.

WOW, SHARP!

Small, sharp teeth lined its jaws all the way to the back of its cheeks. These interlocking teeth acted like a trap for fish and once it got a grip, *Nothosaurus* did not easily let go! It was not a dinosaur at all, in spite of its lizard-like appearance. It is one of a whole group of reptiles called nothosaurs. This group was named by G. von Meunster, in 1834.

SCAN ME
Instructions on page 5

GOOD SWIMMER!

Powerful legs and a strong tail made *Nothosaurus* a very strong swimmer.

LIOPLEURODON

Liopleurodon, meaning 'smooth-sided teeth', lived in the mid-to-late Jurassic Period in what we now know as Europe. *Liopleurodon* had huge flippers that propelled it through the water. It was a successful hunter with a set of long jaws and needle-sharp teeth. It would probably have eaten marine crocodiles, ichthyosaurs and possibly other pliosaurs. Nobody is sure exactly how big *Liopleurodon* was. The largest estimates have it as long as a 25 m (82 ft) swimming pool!

DID YOU KNOW?

As it was a successful hunter, *Liopleurodon* would have had a set of long jaws and needle-sharp teeth. It probably would have preyed on marine crocodiles, giant fish and other pliosaurs.

WHAT'S THAT SMELL?

Liopleurodon had nostrils in its skull, which allowed it to smell its prey in the water.

SHONISAURUS

Shonisaurus, meaning 'lizard from the Shoshone Mountains', lived during the late Triassic Period, around 225–208 million years ago. Like other ichthyosaurs, *Shonisaurus* is believed to have evolved from land-dwelling reptiles that returned to the water. *Shonisaurus* fossils have been found in land-locked Nevada, which was submerged beneath a shallow body of water during much of the Mesozoic Era.

AS BIG AS A WHALE!

Shonisaurus was an ichthyosaur and looked very much like a dolphin. However, its body was a huge 15 m (49 ft) long, so it was more like a whale in size.

BACK PLATES!

Miners discovered the first bones of the *Shonisaurus* and it is thought they used its backbone segments as dinner plates!

105

ATTACK AND DEFENCE

Dinosaurs attacked each other, defended themselves and competed for leadership within groups. Even though some dinosaurs could be deadly, most of them were peaceful herbivores that never attacked. By the end of the Cretaceous Period, after millions of years of being attacked by tyrannosaurs, raptors and other fierce hunters, evolution produced some of the most heavily armoured defensive animals the world has ever seen! These dinosaurs were the ankylosaurs.

SCAN ME
Instructions on page 5

IN THE CORNER FOR ATTACK!

TEETH Most predators would use their teeth as a weapon to maim or kill their prey. *Tyrannosaurus rex* (p30) had 58 serrated teeth which re-grew when damaged, making it a fearsome attacker. Palaeontologists believe that some of *Tyrannosaurus rex*'s teeth were specifically shaped to gather shreds of the meat as it ate. As the meat rotted, it bred dangerous bacteria, meaning a non-fatal bite would result in an infected wound. The prey would then be likely to die from the infection.

CLAWS It's unlikely that a dinosaur would have killed its prey with claws alone. However, the claws would have been used to grab prey and keep it in a death grip. *Baryonyx* in particular had large, powerful claws on its front hands, which it most probably used to slash prey.

EYESIGHT and SMELL *Troodon* (p56) had large eyes and binocular vision, making it easier for it to spot its prey. *Tyrannosaurus rex* had an advanced sense of smell, which allowed it to smell prey from a long distance away.

FORCE An attacking *Tyrannosaurus rex* could knock its victim clean off its feet, provided it had the element of surprise. Once a potential victim was on its back and stunned, the tyrannosaur could move in for the kill.

IN THE CORNER FOR DEFENCE!

TAILS The long, flexible tails of sauropods could be used like whips, delivering stunning blows to approaching predators. *Ankylosaurus* (p110) had the best defensive tail, with its mace-like growth on the end that could crush the skulls and bones of its enemies.

ARMOUR No creature on Earth was more geared up to defend itself from attack than *Ankylosaurus*, who even had armoured eyelids! By the time the dinosaurs became extinct, even some of the sauropods had developed light armour, which may have helped fend off attacks from predators.

SIZE Sauropods grew to such massive sizes that they were virtually immune to predators. Even a pack of adult *Velociraptors* would have had trouble taking down a 110 ton *Argentinosaurus*.

SPEED While the massive sauropods weren't able to run very fast, most of the hadrosaurs could rise onto their back legs and run away. Some smaller plant-eating dinosaurs may have been capable of sprinting at least 30-40 kph (18-25 mph), especially when being chased.

HEARING Generally, predators had superior sight and smell, while prey had acute hearing, so they could run away if they hear an unfamiliar sound. It is known that *Hadrosaurus* (p80) could make sounds and it's likely that they bellowed to each other, warning the entire herd about an approaching threat.

STEGOSAURUS

Stegosaurus is one of the most recognizable dinosaurs. It is famous for its tail spikes and the plates that run along its back. This is how it got its name, meaning 'covered lizard'. *Stegosaurus* was a herbivore and its brain was no larger than a modern-day dog's.

GUESS WHAT?

The *Stegosaurus* featured tail spikes that reached around 60-90 cm (2-3 ft) in length. Along with *Tyrannosaurus rex* and *Iguanodon*, *Stegosaurus* was one of three dinosaurs that inspired the movie, *Godzilla*.

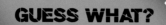

MPH
60 80
40 100
20 120
0 140
000108

AMAZING!

Researchers believe that *Stegosaurus* had a maximum speed of around 7 kph (5 mph). The 17 plates on *Stegosaurus*' back came from its skin, rather than its skeleton. The largest plates were around 60 cm (2 ft) tall and 60 cm (2 ft) wide.

SCAN ME
Instructions on page 5

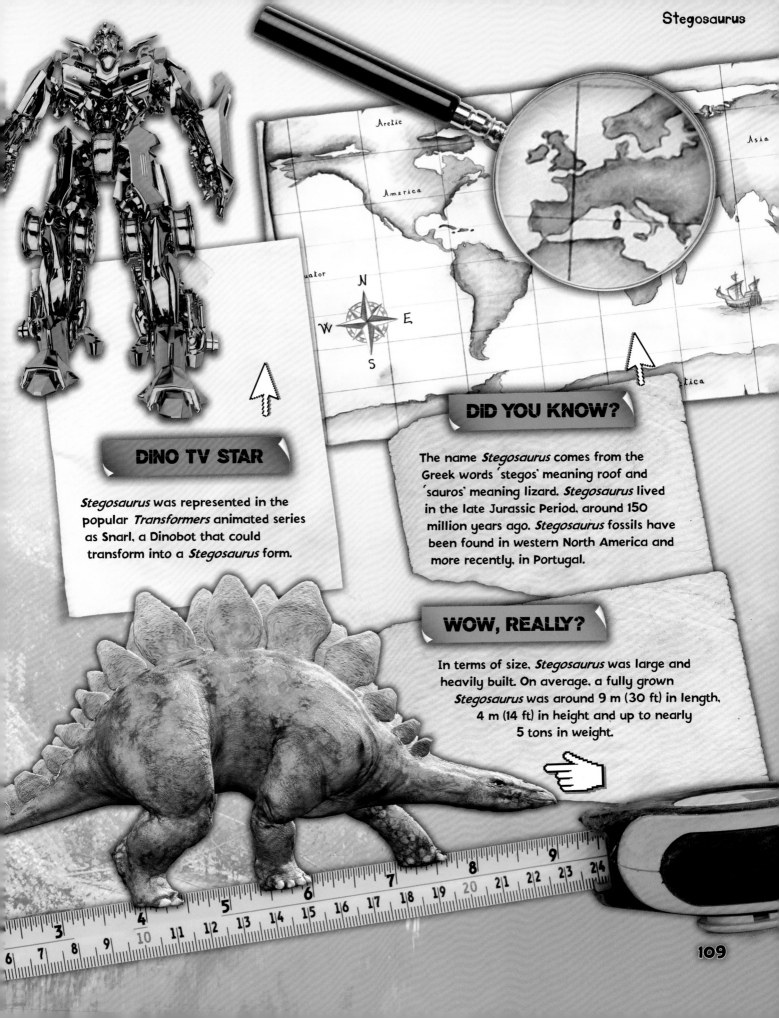

DINO TV STAR

Stegosaurus was represented in the popular *Transformers* animated series as Snarl, a Dinobot that could transform into a *Stegosaurus* form.

DID YOU KNOW?

The name *Stegosaurus* comes from the Greek words ´stegos` meaning roof and ´sauros` meaning lizard. *Stegosaurus* lived in the late Jurassic Period, around 150 million years ago. *Stegosaurus* fossils have been found in western North America and more recently, in Portugal.

WOW, REALLY?

In terms of size, *Stegosaurus* was large and heavily built. On average, a fully grown *Stegosaurus* was around 9 m (30 ft) in length, 4 m (14 ft) in height and up to nearly 5 tons in weight.

ANKYLOSAURUS

Ankylosaurus was a massive, armoured dinosaur which lived during the Cretaceous Period. It was about 7–11 m (23–36 ft) long and would have weighed roughly 3–4 tons. Its armour was really impressive and its name, meaning 'fused lizard', is taken from this. Its back, sides and tail were completely protected. Even its eyelids had plates of bone! It is most famous for its tail club, which would have been used as a defensive weapon. Only its stomach was unarmoured, so flipping it over was the only way it could be wounded.

NOT VERY CLEVER!

As big as *Ankylosaurus* was, it had an unusually small brain. It was about the same size as *Stegosaurus'*, which wasn't the cleverest of dinosaurs!

DID YOU KNOW?

Ankylosaurus was the Cretaceous equivalent of an armoured truck. It was very wide and covered with very thick, almost impenetrable armour.

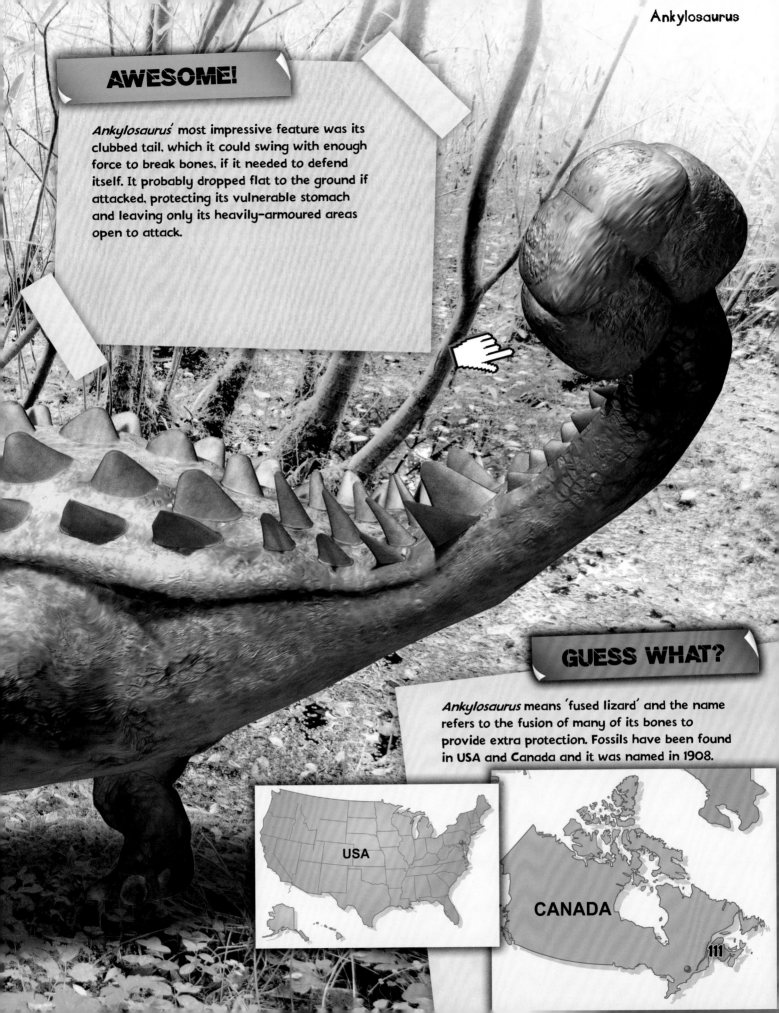

AWESOME!

Ankylosaurus' most impressive feature was its clubbed tail, which it could swing with enough force to break bones, if it needed to defend itself. It probably dropped flat to the ground if attacked, protecting its vulnerable stomach and leaving only its heavily-armoured areas open to attack.

GUESS WHAT?

Ankylosaurus means 'fused lizard' and the name refers to the fusion of many of its bones to provide extra protection. Fossils have been found in USA and Canada and it was named in 1908.

USA

CANADA

111

KENTROSAURUS

Kentrosaurus means 'spiked lizard' and was named after the dramatic double row of bony spikes that ran down its back. It lived during the late Jurassic Period, about 156–150 million years ago. It had a tiny, narrow head, ending in a toothless beak. Small teeth further back in its cheeks helped it to mash up the fern and lush riverside plants it grazed on. *Kentrosaurus* fossils have only ever been found in Tanzania.

TWO BRAINS?!

Kentrosaurus was once believed to have two brains! Scientists now know that the second was merely a group of nerves that controlled the tail and back legs.

HOW DO YOU SAY MY NAME?

KEN-troh-SAW-rus

DID YOU KNOW?

Kentrosaurus grew to around 2.5 m (8 ft) long and would have weighed almost 2 tons. Each of the spikes on *Kentrosaurus'* back were around 30 cm (12 in) high.

WOW, FACT!

Kentrosaurus' olfactory bulbs (the area of the brain controlling smell) were very well-developed, so it had a keen sense of smell.

Its back legs were twice as long as its front legs and it may have been able to stand on its hind legs for short periods of time to reach higher-up vegetation, such as leaves.

EDMONTONIA

Edmontonia means 'from Edmonton', the place where it was found in Alberta, Canada. It lived 76–68 million years ago during the Cretaceous Period. *Edmontonia* was a tank-like dinosaur with a pear-shaped head. It had scutes (bony plates) on its back and head and sharp spikes along its back and tail. Four large spikes stuck out from its shoulders on each side.

WOW, BIG!

Edmontonia was one of the largest nodosaurids at 6–7 m (20–23 ft) in length and weighed in at around 3.5 tons.

LIKE A HELMET

Edmontonia's head was covered in armoured scales to protect its brain. Two collars of flat, bony plates protected the back of the neck.

GOOD DEFENCE

Edmontonia had special shoulder muscles that let it draw in its front legs and hold its body to the ground if it was attacked..

YOU'RE NOT EATING ME!

Slow-moving *Edmontonia* would have needed every bit of its impressive armour, as it lived at the same time as *Tyrannosaurus rex.*

DID YOU KNOW?

Edmontonia had very wide feet which it would have used to walk safely around on wet and marshy ground and not get stuck!

SCELIDOSAURUS

Scelidosaurus, meaning 'limb lizard', was named by Sir Richard Owen in 1868. It lived in the early Jurassic Period, around 206–200 million years ago. *Scelidosaurus* was an armoured, plant-eating dinosaur. It had a small head, stocky legs and a long, stiffened tail. Its fossils have been found in Dorset, England and were very well-preserved.

ANKYLOSAUR OR STEGOSAUR?

Scelidosaurus has been classified at different times as both a stegosaur and an ankylosaur. The bony plates in its skin resemble a later ankylosaur, however, the bony plates down its back and its heavy body are similar to a stegosaur. Scientists still do not wholly agree about which group it belongs to. It is thought *Scelidosaurus* might well have been an ancestor to both.

SLICE AND DICE

Scelidosaurus' narrow beak contained small, leaf-shaped teeth in the front of the upper jaw. These teeth were useful for slicing flowers and fruits off plants, rather than chewing food.

EXTRA LUNCH!

Young *Scelidosaurus* might have eaten insects to add **extra protein** to its diet.

DID YOU KNOW?

Scelidosaurus was one of the first of the armoured dinosaurs. It was around 3-4 m (10-13 ft) long and weighed about 200-250 kg (440-550 lbs).

117

SCUTELLOSAURUS

Scutellosaurus means 'little shield lizard' and it gets its name from the bony armour 'shields' called scutes that covered its tiny body. It lived in what is now North America, in the early Jurassic Period. *Scutellosaurus* was a plant-eater and spent much of its time grazing. Its back legs were much longer than its front ones and scientists believe it walked on four legs most of the time. However, if attacked, it could rise up onto its back legs and run away at a decent speed.

WOW, REALLY?

When we think of dinosaurs, especially armoured ones, we tend to think of massive creatures, but *Scutellosaurus* weighed no more than a medium-sized dog at around 10 kg (22 lbs)!

LONG TAIL!

Scutellosaurus had a short skull. Its tail, on the other hand, was twice the length of its body and head put together.

TWO OR FOUR LEGS?

Scutellosaurus was a creature that could walk on either two legs, or on all four legs. This meant *Scutellosaurus was* 'semi-bipedal'. Its own ancestors had been fully bipedal (walking on two legs) and its descendants would be quadrupeds (walking on four legs).

DID YOU KNOW?

More than 300 scutes protected *Scutellosaurus*. These ran along its back and tail. Six different types of bony plates have been found, the largest of which would have formed one or two rows down the centre of its back. Any predator trying to take a bite out of this little guy would have been in for a shock!

GUESS WHAT?

Fossils have been found in Arizona, North America, but little is really known about this dinosaur, as only two incomplete skeletons have been found.

NODOSAURUS

Nodosaurus means 'knobbed lizard' and it takes its name from the bony armour plates and knobs which covered most of its skin. It lived during the Cretaceous Period, around 110 million years ago. It gave its name to the group of ankylosaurs called nodosaurids and fossils have been found in North America. It was a plant-eater and may have also swallowed small stones to aid in grinding up food in its large gut. Unlike other ankylosaurs, *Nodosaurus* did not have a club on its tail, so when attacked, it probably dropped flat to the ground, a bit like a hedgehog!

NOT THE CLEVEREST!

Compared to the size of its body, *Nodosarus* had a small head and miniscule brain, indicating very low intelligence.

GUESS WHAT?

Nodosaurus (pronounced NOH-doh-SAW-rus) was one of the earliest armoured dinosaurs discovered. It was first identified by Othniel Charles Marsh who discovered parts of it, in 1889. Fossils have been found in Kansas and Wyoming, North America.

DID YOU KNOW?

Nodosaurus was similar to a modern day rhinoceros, in that it spent its life moving slowly through the grasslands, grazing for food.

ARMOUR WAS ITS ONLY DEFENCE!

Nodosaurus had little means of attacking an enemy. If threatened, it probably relied on crouching low to the ground to protect its soft underside.

121

MINMI

Minmi was an unusually small and primitive ankylosaur, with a tiny brain. It walked on four short legs and it had a short neck, wide skull and a long tail. A plant-eater, it lived during the early Cretaceous Period, about 119–113 million years ago. It was discovered at Minmi Crossing, in Australia. *Minmi* had extra bony plates on its backbone. These strengthened its back, helping to support the weight of its armour. Extra muscles attached to these extra plates could have allowed *Minmi* to run at a reasonable speed.

WOW, FACT!

Minmi was about 3 m (10 ft) long and was roughly 1 m (3 ft) tall to the top of its shoulder. It would have been roughly the same size as a one year-old calf.

COOL!

Minmi had skin armoured with large, bony plates and smaller pea-sized bones called ossicles embedded all over it. Even *Minmi's* underbelly was protected by small bony plates, which makes it unique among the thyreophoran group of dinosaurs.

WHAT'S IN A NAME?

Minmi has the shortest name ever given to a dinosaur. *Minmi*, pronounced MIN-mee, was named after Minmi Crossing in Australia.

DOWN UNDER!

Minmi was the first armoured dinosaur found south of the equator. It is also the most complete dinosaur skeleton ever found in Australia. The first fossils were discovered by Alan Batholomai near Roma, Queensland in 1964.

DID YOU KNOW?

Some scientists have suggested that some of the horizontal bones in *Minmi's* back are actually tendons which have ossified (changed into bone), rather than true bones.

EGGS AND LIFE CYCLE

Dinosaur eggs were hard-shelled eggs, much like those of reptiles and birds today, laid by the females. They came in a variety of shapes and sizes, some as big as 60 cm (24 in) long. Even the largest of eggs would have needed the shell to be thin enough to allow oxygen in and to allow the baby dinosaur to get out. Some dinosaurs would have cared for their young, but others would have abandoned them as soon as they were born. Very little is known about the family lifestyle of dinosaurs, although some evidence found in the Gobi Desert in the 1920s showed tracks of adults and babies moving together.

NESTS

Dinosaurs scraped nests into the ground. These ranged from simple pits dug into the earth, to more elaborately designed nests with mud rims. Sometimes, depending on the species of dinosaur, nests appeared in large nesting grounds.

FIRST EGG!

The first fossilized dinosaur egg was found in France, in 1869, and was laid by *Hypselosaurus*, a member of the titanosaur family.

HOW ON EARTH!

One of the biggest unanswered questions about dinosaur eggs is: how did the giant sauropods such as *Apatosaurus* and *Diplodocus* lay their eggs without breaking them? Given the massive size of these creatures, even if they squatted while laying their eggs, the eggs would have still dropped from a height of around 2.5 m (8 ft) and would have been unlikely to survive. Some scientists have argued that sauropods may have had an extendable tube for laying eggs, like some modern-day turtles have.

WOW, FACT!

Dinosaurs appeared to have a homing instinct much like a pigeon or a swallow, that would guide them back, year after year, to the same breeding grounds.

DID YOU KNOW?

More than 200 dinosaur egg sites have been found around the world.

125

DIMORPHODON

Dimorphodon is one of the earliest flying reptiles ever discovered. It belongs to the pterosaur family and lived during the early Jurassic Period. *Dimorphodon* means 'two-form teeth', in reference to the distinct types of teeth in its jaw. This is a rare feature among reptiles. It was discovered in Dorset, England. This area is now known as the Jurassic Coast. *Dimorphodon* flew well, using large, lightweight wings. Its long, thin tail with a diamond-shaped flap of skin at the end, helped stabilize it during flight. Many believe it had a beak like a puffin!

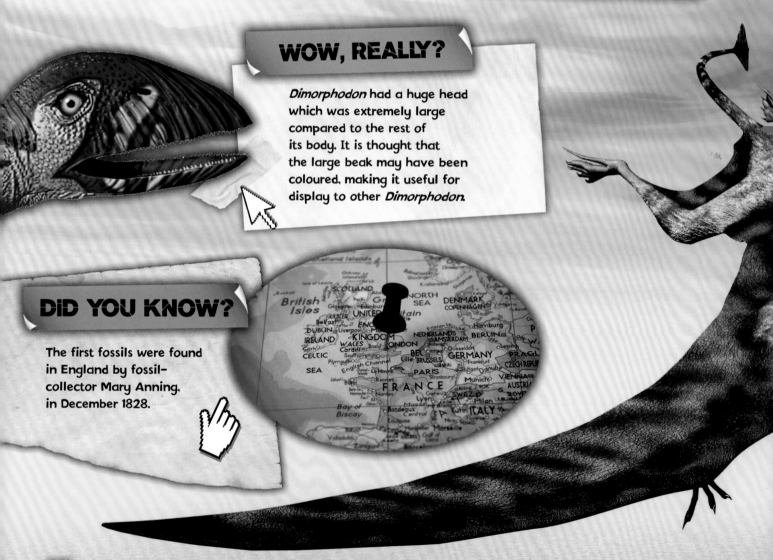

WOW, REALLY?

Dimorphodon had a huge head which was extremely large compared to the rest of its body. It is thought that the large beak may have been coloured, making it useful for display to other *Dimorphodon*.

DID YOU KNOW?

The first fossils were found in England by fossil-collector Mary Anning, in December 1828.

Dimorphodon

GUESS WHAT?

Unlike most other pterosaurs, *Dimorphodon* had legs which stuck out to the sides. These would have made it walk with a clumsy waddle!

HOW DO YOU SAY MY NAME?

Die-MORF-oh-don

COOL!

Palaeontologists suggest that *Dimorphodon* would have been able to run very fast by rising up onto its toes.

127

CAUDIPTERYX

Caudipteryx was a small, bipedal dinosaur. Its name means 'tail feather' and refers to its feathered tail plume. Its teeth were long and sharp and its long legs would have made it a very fast runner. *Caudipteryx* was the size of a peacock and very much resembled a bird, but it could not fly. The discovery of *Caudipteryx* sparked an important debate about the relationship between birds and dinosaurs.

WOW, REALLY?

Some scientists think that *Caudipteryx* proves that birds descended from dinosaurs. Its feathers suggest that it might be the missing link in the evolution of dinosaurs to birds.

DID YOU KNOW?

Caudipteryx was approximately 1 m (3 ft) long and weighed in at about 9 kg (20 lbs) - that's the same weight as a turkey!

GUESS WHAT?

Philip Currie identified the fossils in 1997, in China.

COOL!

Caudipteryx's teeth faced outwards, giving it a distinctly buck-toothed appearance. It is possible it had a diet consisting of plants, small fish and other small animals.

129

ARCHAEOPTERYX

Archaeopteryx means 'ancient feather', but is sometimes referred to by its German name, Urvogel. This means 'original bird'. It lived in the Jurassic Period, around 150 million years ago. It resembled a magpie or raven in size, but had the bone structure of a dinosaur. *Archaeopteryx* is generally considered to be an important link between dinosaurs and birds.

WOW, REALLY?

Archaeopteryx's inner ear was very similar to a modern-day bird's and the areas of its brain controlling movement and vision were enlarged. That's why we can say that *Archaeopteryx*'s brain was designed for flight and balance!

DINOSAUR AND BIRD?

Archaeopteryx is often said to be a link between dinosaurs and birds.

BIRD-LIKE FEATURES
Feathered wings with reduced fingers
Bird-like brain
Feathers on body and tail
Wishbone
Hollow bones
Long, bony tail

DINOSAUR-LIKE FEATURES
Claws on wings could be used to grasp
Long bony tail
Teeth
Jaws (not a beak!)

DID YOU KNOW?

Archaeopteryx had large eyes which would have given it excellent vision.

GUESS WHAT?

Ever since the first *Archaeopteryx* was found, scientists have argued over whether or not this animal could fly. Studies into an *Achaeopteryx*'s brain by Dr Angela Milner have led to the belief that it did indeed fly, but not very well!

PTERANODON

Pteranodon was not a dinosaur, but a massive flying reptile. It takes its name from the Greek for 'winged' and 'toothless'. It lived near the coast during the Cretaceous Period. Even though it had no teeth, it was perfectly evolved for fishing straight from the surface of the water. It had excellent eyesight and a scooped beak.

WOW, REALLY?

Pteranodon would have been agile, elegant and quite fast when flying, reaching speeds of up to 48 kph (30 mph).

60
80
40
MPH
100
20
120
0
000108
140

HOW DO YOU SAY MY NAME?

TEH-ran-uh-don

DID YOU KNOW?

Pteranodon's lower jaw was over 1 m (3 ft) long. It had a wingspan of up to 9–10 m (30–33 ft) and it would have weighed around 20–25 kg (44–55 lbs).

COOL!

Pteranodon probably looked more like a giant bat than a bird, with large, soft, hair-covered membranes for wings which were very thin, but extremely strong. This reptile did not have any feathers.

WALKED AND FLEW!

Pteranodon would have been able to walk on the ground, but once in the air, it would have looked like a huge glider. It would have been able to fly long distances using its lightweight wings.

GUESS WHAT?

Pteranodon had a long head crest that was probably used to help counter-balance the weight of its massive beak.

RHAMPHORHYNCHUS

Rhamphorhynchus means 'beak snout' and it was a pterosaur that lived during the late Jurassic Period. It had a long, stiff tail and a wingspan up to 1.8 m (6 ft). *Rhamphorhynchus* fed by dipping its head into the lakes and rivers of what is now Europe. It would scoop up wriggling fish, thanks to its narrow beak and sharp teeth. Its tiny legs meant *Rhamphorhynchus* wouldn't have hunted on land, because it would have been a poor runner. Many believe *Rhamphorhynchus* was nocturnal like some modern-day seabirds.

WOW, REALLY?

Rhamphorhynchus had thin, long jaws with amazingly sharp teeth. It is believed that it hunted by dragging its beak in the water in the hope of coming into contact with fish, then it would snap its needle-sharp teeth shut and toss the food into its throat pouch.

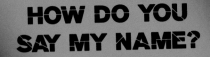

HOW DO YOU SAY MY NAME?

RAM-for-INK-us

DIAMOND TAIL

At the end of its tail, it had a flap of skin, which was diamond-shaped.

DID YOU KNOW?

This pterosaur was less than 30 cm (12 in) long, but its wings, when fully extended, stretched up to 90 cm (3 ft) from tip to tip.

GUESS WHAT?

Rhamphorhynchus fossils have been recovered from Jurassic marine clays in southern England and Portugal, but the finest specimens come from the Solnhofen quarry in Bavaria, southern Germany.

PTEROSAURS

Pterosaur means 'winged lizard' and they were a group of closely related flying reptiles that lived from the late Triassic Period to the end of the Cretaceous Period, 228–65 million years ago. The evidence for their ability to fly comes from their light, hollow bones, large brains and an extremely long fourth digit that provided wing support. Pterosaur fossils have shown they would have had hair, so they would also have been warm-blooded. They would have lived on a diet of fish, molluscs and insects.

WOW, REALLY?

Pterosaurs had large brains and good eyesight.

DID YOU KNOW?

Pterosaur wings were covered with a leathery and tough membrane that stretched between its body, the top of its legs and its fourth finger.

WRONG DINO!

Not all pterosaurs are the same. There were many different types of pterosaurs and their wing designs differed. This meant that some of the species flapped their wings and could fly with great power, while others simply glided through the air, relying on updrafts of warm air to help them fly.

IT IS A DUCK OR A BIRD?

When pterosaurs were first discovered, it was thought that they lived in water, possibly because some species had webbed feet. However, in the 19th century, George Cuvier proposed that pterosaurs flew.

EXTRA LUNCH!

Young pterosaurs may have added extra protein to their diet by eating insects.

QUETZALCOATLUS

Quetzalcoatlus is one of the largest flying animals to have ever lived on Earth. It was a member of a family of advanced, toothless pterosaurs with unusually long necks. Its beak was sharp and pointed and at the front of its wings, there were three-fingered hands that had sharp claws. *Quetzalcoatlus* was named in 1975, after the Aztec feathered serpent god, Quetzalcoatl. It lived at the same time as *Triceratops* and *Tyrannosaurus rex. Quetzalcoatlus* became extinct at the end of the Cretaceous Period, 65 million years ago.

WOW, REALLY?

It weighed the same as an adult human, around 70 kg (154 lbs).

My objective

HOW DO YOU SAY MY NAME?

KWET-zal-koh-AT-luss

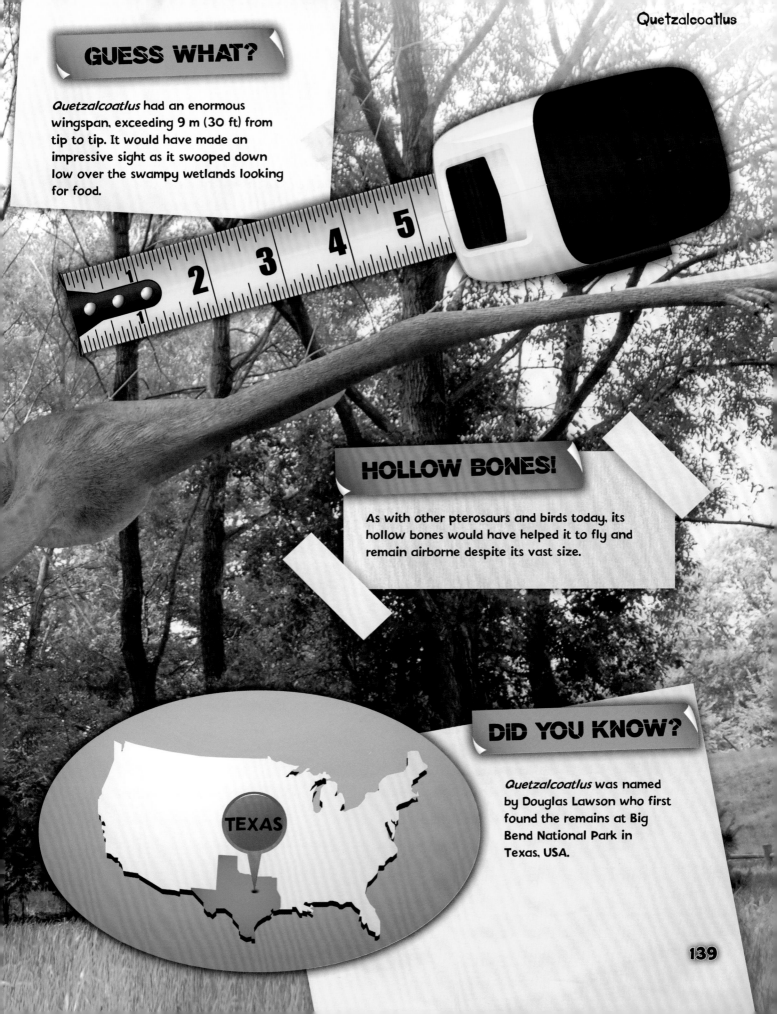

GUESS WHAT?

Quetzalcoatlus had an enormous wingspan, exceeding 9 m (30 ft) from tip to tip. It would have made an impressive sight as it swooped down low over the swampy wetlands looking for food.

HOLLOW BONES!

As with other pterosaurs and birds today, its hollow bones would have helped it to fly and remain airborne despite its vast size.

DID YOU KNOW?

Quetzalcoatlus was named by Douglas Lawson who first found the remains at Big Bend National Park in Texas, USA.

TEXAS

TROPEOGNATHUS

Tropeognathus means 'keel jaw', taken from the bumps found on its beak. It is thought to have lived near coastal waters, where it hunted fish and other animals living in the shallow waters. *Tropeognathus* lived during the Cretaceous Period and had a wingspan of up to 6 m (20 ft) wide. It was lightweight enough to prey on fish and squid, while hovering at the surface of lakes and swamps. It had around 48 teeth in total for catching, killing and eating its prey. It also had a crest bone to stabilize its head. Palaeontologists believe *Tropeognathus* would travel large distances searching for food, using warm thermals to take off and soar through the air.

WOW, REALLY?

Tropeognathus was very large. Its wingspan was nearly 6 m (20 ft) wide. That is longer than three fully grown men!

GUESS WHAT?

Tropeognathus had large bumps on the top and bottom of its beak. Scientists believe that this may have helped *Tropeognathus* remain stable as it flew over the water, dragging its beak under the surface.

COOL!

Tropeognathus could feed like a flamingo trailing its beak in the water.

DID YOU KNOW?

Tropeognathus fossils were discovered in rocks in the Santana Formation in north-eastern Brazil and have been very precisely dated to 115 million years ago.

Venezuela

• Manaus

Brazil

SANTANA FORMATION

Bolivia
La Paz

• Brasilia

Paraguay
Asuncion

Sao Paulo •

Argentina

Uruguay
Buenos Aires • Montevideo

YOU CAN'T CATCH ME!

Tropeognathus tended to remain near water, resting on cliffs as it went, but rarely ventured very far inland as it might get hunted.

TRICERATOPS

Triceratops is one of the most famous of all the dinosaurs. This is probably because of its 'three-horned face' from which it takes its name. It lived in what is now North America in the late Cretaceous Period, about 72–65 million years ago. This was during the Age of Reptiles, at the end of the Mesozoic Era. *Triceratops* was a plant-eater and probably used its powerful beak to crush food, such as cycads and other low-lying plants. *Triceratops* walked on four short legs and would have been a relatively slow dinosaur.

BIG HEAD!

Triceratops had one of the largest skulls of any land animal discovered so far. Some skulls measured a massive 3 m (10 ft) in length.

WOW FACT!

Although the name *Triceratops* means 'three-horned face', not all specimens had three horns. Often the nasal horn was either very short or nearly absent. However, the two brow horns, which grew out of the top of the skull over each eye, were always large and well developed.

MEGA BUCKS!

One reason *Triceratops* is so well known is because of its large, bony skull, which fossilized fairly easily and often in one piece. For this reason, complete *Triceratops* skulls have become prized items at auctions worldwide, fetching millions of dollars from wealthy bidders. The most famous recent example is a *Triceratops* called Cliff, who was purchased for $1 million in 2008 by a wealthy dinosaur fan and donated to the Boston Museum of Science.

WOW, MISTAKE!

The palaeontologist who named *Triceratops* thought it was an ancient Bison. In 1887, Othniel C. Marsh examined a *Triceratops*' skull, complete with horns and assigned the remains to the grazing mammal *bison alticornis*, which didn't evolve until tens of millions of years later. Fortunately for his reputation, Marsh quickly reversed the error.

PROTOCERATOPS

Protoceratops means 'first horned face'. It lived in the scrublands and deserts of what is now Asia in the late Cretaceous Period, around 85–70 million years ago. It was a plant-eater that was around the size of a modern-day sheep. *Protoceratops* walked on four legs and had a large head, a bulky body and a parrot-like beak. Most notably, it had a large frill on its head. This was probably used for display rather than defence. *Protoceratops* lacked any well developed horns, compared to its later descendants. Some believe that *Protoceratops* was the basis for a mythical creature known as a griffin.

DID YOU KNOW?

Whenever palaeontologists discover multiple fossils of a dinosaur genus in any given location, the most logical conclusion is usually that this creature roamed in packs or herds. It's likely that *Protoceratops* travelled in herds of hundreds, perhaps even thousands, of individuals.

HOW DO YOU SAY MY NAME?

pro-toe-SAIR-uh-tops

NOT AS BIG AS YOU THINK!

Protoceratops is one of those dinosaurs that people think was a lot bigger than it actually was. Today, it's often mistakenly pictured as a giant, but this horned dinosaur was only about 2 m (6 ft) in length and 75 cm (30 in) high. The recorded weights for *Protoceratops* vary, but it is thought to be around 400 kg (880 lbs).

WOW, FAMOUS!

Protoceratops has earned a place in the palaeontology hall of fame for a rare fossil find, in 1971 in the Gobi Desert. Scientists found the tangled skeletons of a *Protoceratops* and a *Velociraptor*, who were thought to be in mid-fight when they were both buried together by a sudden sandstorm, preserving their battle forever!

MICROCERATUS

Microceratus, meaning 'small horned face', is one of the the smallest known horned dinosaurs. A ceratopsian dinosaur, it was a plant-eater, found in what is now Asia and North America. It lived around 70 million years ago, in the late Cretaceous Period. Microceratops was only 0.6 m (2 ft) high and was both small and lightly built. This probably made *Microceratus* very agile and fast. Its back legs were longer than its front legs, allowing it to balance and hop on the hind legs. Information about *Microceratus* is based on very limited fossil remains, so there's still a lot we don't know about this dinosaur. *Microceratus* did not have any horns, but it did have the obvious head frill and beak-like mouth so common with horned dinosaurs.

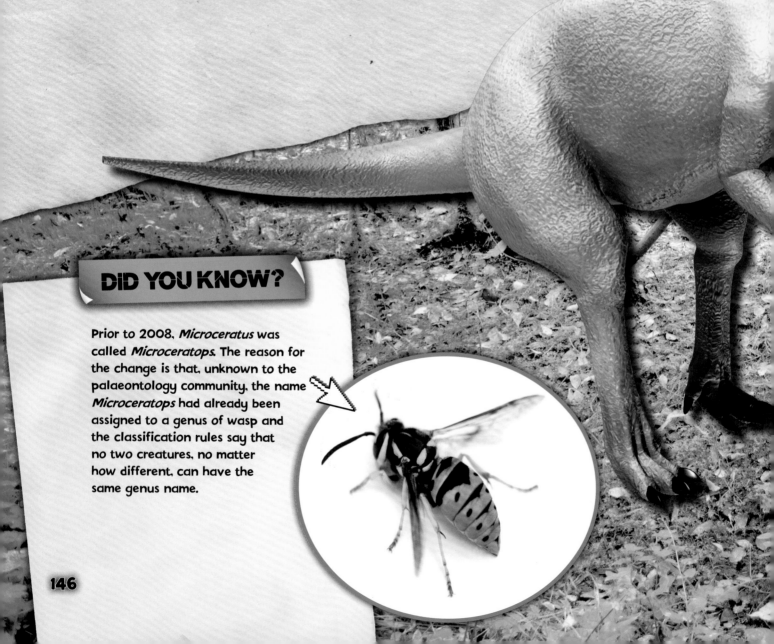

DID YOU KNOW?

Prior to 2008, *Microceratus* was called *Microceratops*. The reason for the change is that, unknown to the palaeontology community, the name *Microceratops* had already been assigned to a genus of wasp and the classification rules say that no two creatures, no matter how different, can have the same genus name.

WHERE WAS MICROCERATUS FOUND?

Microceratus was discovered in 1953 in Mongolia. Subsequently, additional fossils have been found in Mongolia and also in China.

SMALL, BUT NOT THAT SMALL!

Microceratus was not quite the smallest dinosaur that ever lived – that was *Compsognathus longipes*, which was only the size of a chicken.

AWESOME!

Microceratus appeared as part of the herd in the Walt Disney film *Dinosaur* (2000).

LEPTOCERATOPS

Leptoceratops, meaning 'lean-horned face' lived on the plains of western North America in the late Cretaceous Period, around 70 million years ago.

A plant-eater, *Leptoceratops* had a small head frill and no horns. It usually walked on all fours, but could also stand and run on two legs. Its front digits had the ability to grasp and were probably used to pull branches and other food towards its mouth. It would also have used its sharp, parrot-shaped beak to slice off leaves. *Leptoceratops* was around 2.4 m (8 ft) long.

LOOK AFTER THOSE TEETH!

Leptoceratops' teeth were different to those of its fellow ceratopsians. They were broad instead of long, which may have helped it chew up all kinds of different vegetation. They had single roots, and each tooth had only one replacement tooth available. Most ceratopsians had several teeth ready to take the place of one that was broken or fell out.

DID YOU KNOW?

Leptoceratops was discovered in 1924 by Barnum Brown in North America. Scientists believe that *Leptoceratops* was a late-surviving, primitive, horned dinosaur. More recently, fossilized *Leptoceratops* bones have been found in Australia, showing that they may have lived all over the world.

A LONG STROLL

Fossil finds in Australia date from the early Cretaceous Period, whereas all previous finds dated from towards the end of the period. It seems *Leptoceratops* may have walked the Earth for some 50 million years!

149

CENTROSAURUS

Centrosaurus means 'pointed lizard' and was a four-legged, plant-eating dinosaur. *Centrosaurus* lived in herds during the late Cretaceous Period, roughly 76 million years ago, in the woodlands of what is now western North America. *Centosaurus* was about 6 m (20 ft) long, 1.8 m (6 ft) tall and would have weighed about 3 tons.

Centrosaurus was the first of the 'short-frilled' ceratops to be discovered and is distinguished by its two large hornlets, which hook over its frill.

IMPRESSIVE HORN!

Centrosaurus' most distinctive feature was its impressive horn growing from its nose, which was 46 cm (18 in) long! In different species of *Centrosaurus*, this horn curved either forward or backwards.

SCAN ME
Instructions on page 5

DIET

Low lying plants.

LOST RELATIVES!

Recently, palaeontologists announced a find of a pair of new ceratopsians that seem to have been closely related to *Centrosaurus*, the North American *Diabloceratops* and *Medusaceratops*, both of which had unique horn and frill combinations reminiscent of their more famous cousin.

SKELETONS

The study of all dinosaurs starts with the skeletons. Anatomically, dinosaurs have skeletal features which help scientists to identify them as dinosaurs. Most skeletons are discovered from excavated dinosaur fossils. Unless a complete skeleton is found, which is rare, scientists have to reference information from other fossil finds, or make an educated guess using scientific software as to what the dinosaur would have looked like.

WHAT MAKES A DINOSAUR A DINOSAUR?

Dinosaurs are classified by their hip structure. This is important because dinosaurs, unlike reptiles whose legs sprawl out to the side, walked with their legs under their bodies. Dinosaurs have two types of hip structure: lizard-hipped and bird-hipped. Dinosaurs also have a reduced fourth and fifth digit on their hands and their feet have three large toes.

ALL DINOSAURS ARE NOT THE SAME!

Different shaped dinosaurs have different skeletal structures, for example, *Tyrannosaurus rex* (see page 30) was large and bulky, with a big head and powerful jaws. It would have only been able to move quickly over short distances. However, *Hypsilophodon* (see page 162) had a slimmed down structure, like a gazelle, giving it maximum support, but minimum weight so it could run fast over long distances.

SKULL FACT

The shape of a dinosaur's skull, as well as the size, shape and arrangement of its teeth, can tell palaeontologists a lot about its diet. One of the biggest skulls ever found belonged to *Torosaurus* and was 2.5 m (8 ft) long.

BONE CLUES

Skeletons also give scientists an idea of the size of a dinosaur and what it would have looked like. If you stood next to *Brachiosaurus'* leg you would hardly reach its knees!

DINO TWEET

Sue, the largest and most complete *Tyrannosaurus rex* skeleton in the world, is on permanent exhibition at The Field Museum in Chicago, USA. Dinosaur Sue even has her own Twitter account @SUEtheTrex.

DID YOU KNOW

The first near-complete skeleton of a dinosaur was discovered by William Parker Foulke in 1858. It was of a *Hadrosaurus.*

IGUANODON

Iguanodon, meaning 'iguana tooth', was a plant-eating dinosaur that had a conical spike on each thumb. This 9 m (30 ft) long dinosaur lived during the early Cretaceous Period, about 140–110 million years ago.
The supercontinent, Pangaea, was breaking up at this time, but *Iguanodon* still managed to spread to all the modern-day continents, except Antarctica. It was the second type of dinosaur to be formally named. *Iguanodon* could run on two legs or walk on four legs. It had a flat, stiff tail and three-toed hind feet.

IGUANODON STATS

NAME:	*Iguanodon*
PRONUNCIATION:	ig-WAN-oh-don
HEIGHT:	5 m (16 ft)
LENGTH:	9 m (30 ft)
DIET:	Cycads, conifers and ginkgos
LIVED:	110 million years ago
PERIOD:	Early Cretaceous
FEATURES:	Three-toed bird limbs, powerful arms, horse-like skull with toothless beak.

LONG TONGUE

Iguanodon probably nipped prehistoric plants with its tough, toothed beak. It had no teeth in the front of its mouth, but had strong teeth, 5 cm (2 in) long, in the side of its jaw, which it used to grind up tough plant material. Muscle attachment areas inside its head suggest that it may have had a long tongue.

SUPER FACT

Iguanodon bones have been found on nearly every continent of the world.

WOW, FACT!

Iguanodon's outstanding feature was a five-fingered hand made up of a spiked thumb used for defence or perhaps foraging, three middle fingers and a fifth finger for grabbing.

DID YOU KNOW?

Iguanodon (pronounced 'ig-WAN-oh-don') was one of the first dinosaurs to be discovered. The name is from 'iguana', a type of modern reptile and 'don', meaning tooth. *Iguanodon* was named by Gideon A. Mantell in 1825. Its teeth and a few bones were found in 1822 in Sussex, England.

155

GALLIMIMUS

Gallimimus, meaning 'chicken mimic', was the largest-known of the ornithomimids. It has been found only in the late Cretaceous Period, in Mongolia and lived about 75–70 million years ago. *Gallimimus* was a fast-running dinosaur with a small head and a fairly large brain. Its horny beak was long, thin and surprisingly toothless. It had a long neck, tail and legs. It measured around 4–6 m (13–20 ft) long and had large eyes positioned on opposite sides of its head.

DID YOU KNOW?

Gallimimus had short arms with three-clawed fingers on each hand and long legs with three-clawed toes. A long tail acted as a counterbalance and kept it upright during fast turns.

WOW, SPEEDY!

Gallimimus walked on two long, slender legs. It was a fast, agile dinosaur, probably running about as fast as an ostrich can run, which is up to 70 kph (43 mph).

GREEDY DINO

Gallimimus may have been an omnivore, eating small animals, insects, eggs and some plant material, by sieving them from mud with comb-like plates in its mouth. The bottom part of its beak was shaped like a shovel.

157

DRINKER

Drinker was named after Edward Drinker Cope who discovered it. It lived around 150 million years ago during the late Jurassic Period. It was a small, plant-eating dinosaur, which lived near swamps. *Drinker* was only about 2 m (6.5 ft) long, or about the size of a full-grown man. *Drinker* had unusually broad feet and long, wide-spread toes, which may have evolved to negotiate a swampy habitat within Wyoming's late Jurassic Morrison Formation where fossils were found. *Drinker* was very similar to *Othnielia*, which was also named after its discoverer, who was Cope's rival.

WOW, FACT!

The palaentologist Bob Bakker has reported finding the remains of over 30 *Drinker* dinosaurs in what might have been a burrow (though, of course, it could have just been a hole). All known specimens have a floppy tail. This is the tail of choice for negotiating tight tunnel bends.

Drinker

'THE BONE WARS'

In the late 19th century, Edward Drinker Cope and Othniel C. Marsh were big enemies, trying to get one-up on each other on their palaeontological digs, by fair means or foul! They spied, sabotaged and openly slandered each other at every given opportunity. That's why it's ironic that the small, two-legged ornithopod *Drinker* (named after Cope) may be exactly the same animal as the small, two-legged ornithopod *Othnielia* (named after Marsh). The differences between these dinosaurs are so minimal that they may one day be collapsed into the same genus.

159

CAMPTOSAURUS

Camptosaurus, meaning 'flexible lizard', was a plant-eater from the late Jurassic Period and lived around 156–145 million years ago.

Camptosaurus looked a lot like *Iguanodon*. It was a heavy dinosaur, about 5–7 m (16–23 ft) long and 1 m (3.3 ft) high at the hips, weighing roughly 1000 kg (2200 lbs). It had a long snout, hundreds of teeth and a horny beak. Its legs were longer than its arms and it had four-toed feet and five-fingered arms, all with hooves. It could walk on two or four legs and probably spent most of its time grazing for low-lying plants.

DID YOU KNOW?

Camptosaurus was first discovered in 1879 by palaeontologist Earl Douglass in Utah, USA. That same year, this new dinosaur was given the name *Camptonotus* by Othniel Charles Marsh. It was later renamed in 1885 by Marsh because its original name already belonged to a type of cricket.

WHY WAS IT CALLED THAT?

Camptosaurus fed with its short front legs on the ground and the tall hips and rounded curve of the tail gave it a curved or bent profile. This is why it got its name, which means 'flexible lizard'.

AWESOME!

Camptosaurus was one of the earliest ornithopods discovered. It suffered the fate of living with more dinosaurs than could comfortably fit. For this reason, it's now believed that only one identified fossil specimen was a true *Camptosaurus*. The others may well have been species of *Iguanodon*, which lived much later, during the Cretaceous Period.

HYPSILOPHODON

Hypsilophodon roamed Earth during the early Cretaceous Period, around 125 million years ago. It was first discovered in England, on the Isle of Wight. Its name means 'high-ridged teeth', though 'high-ridged' is thought to refer to *Hypsilophodon*'s frill, rather than its teeth. *Hypsilophodon* measured about 2 m (6.5 ft) long and 60 cm (24 in) tall, weighing about 68 kg (150 lbs). *Hypsilophodon* had a beak made of horn, cheek pouches and 28-30 self-sharpening cheek teeth in a small skull. It had large eyes, strong jaws, five-fingered hands and four-toed feet.

DID YOU KNOW?

Hypsilophodon, pronounced HIP-sill-OWE-foe-don, was discovered in 1869 by Gideon Mantall on England's Isle of Wight, or 'Dinosaur Island'. The name *Hypsilophodon* probably refers to the dinosaur's neck frill as well as its teeth, which allowed it to grind up its food prior to swallowing it. This smaller dinosaur is one of very few prehistoric reptiles to have had cheeks, a feature that allowed it to keep food stored in its mouth while it chewed, similar to how humans chew food today.

PEOPLE USED TO THINK...

For years, scientists believed that *Hypsilophodon* may have lived in trees. However, this theory is no longer accepted today as accurate.

TINY!

Hypsilophodon was one of the smallest of all the dinosaurs that ever lived.

ON TWO LEGS

Hypsilophodon was bipedal, meaning that it walked on two legs. It also had small forelimbs.

THESCELOSAURUS

Thescelosaurus, Greek for 'godlike lizard' and pronounced THES-kel-oh-SAWR-us, lived in the woodlands of what is now North America. It lived during the late Cretaceous Period, about 70–65 million years ago. *Thescelosaurus* was about 4 m (13 ft) long and weighed around 300 kg (600 lbs). It was an unusual dinosaur for all sorts of reasons. Despite living towards the end of the Cretaceous Period, just before the dinosaurs became extinct, *Thescelosaurus* was relatively unevolved for an ornithopod. It had short legs, four-toed feet and three different kinds of teeth. Judging by its anatomy, palaeontologists speculate that *Thescelosaurus* couldn't have run very fast. It is not known how it avoided the raptors and tyrannosaurs that populated late Cretaceous North America.

WOW, FACT!

What made *Thescelosaurus* truly famous was the 1993 discovery of an almost intact specimen, containing the fossilized remains of a mammalian-looking, four-chambered heart. The trouble is, palaeontologists are now divided over whether this was really the dinosaur's heart or some by-product of the fossilization process that has nothing to do with *Thescelosaurus'* anatomy. The evidence is still inconclusive.

AWESOME!

Thescelosaurus was discovered in 1891. However, this dinosaur did not receive a name until 1913. After being discovered, the fossils were hidden away in a crate, in the basement of the Smithsonian Institution, until they were studied many years later by American palaeontologist, Charles Gilmore.

DIET

Thescelosaurus only ate plants, making it a herbivore.

DID YOU KNOW?

Small, scaly plates running along *Thescelosaurus'* back would have protected it from attack.

TENONTOSAURUS

Tenontosaurus, meaning 'tendon lizard', was a medium-sized, bird-footed, ornithopod. Living in the early Cretaceous Period, 120 million years ago, this plant-eater is most famous for its long tail, held off the ground by strong tendons. It would have weighed about 1-2 tons. *Tenontosaurus* was discovered in North America and named in 1970, by palaeontologist, John Ostrom.

WOW, FACT!

Tenontosaurus was most interesting for its unusually long and broad tail. Its tail was suspended off the ground and stiffened by special, bony tendons, which ran all down *Tenontosaurus'* back and along the tail itself.

DID YOU KNOW?

Tenontosaurus probably walked on all fours and ate low-growing plants and shrubs.

WOW, TASTY!

Some dinosaurs are more famous for how they got eaten, than for how they actually lived. That's the case with *Tenontosaurus*, as it was often prey for the small raptor *Deinonychus*. An adult *Tenontosaurus* was large, around 1000 kg (2000 lbs) and smaller raptors such as *Deinonychus* would have hunted in packs to bring it down.

TENONTOSAURUS STATS

PRONUNCIATION:	teh-NON-tuh-SAWR-us
HEIGHT:	3-4 m (10-13 ft)
LENGTH:	7 m (23 ft)
DIET:	Low-lying ferns
LIVED:	120-100 million years ago
PERIOD:	Middle Cretaceous Period

ORMATION OF FOSSILS

A fossil is a trace of past life, preserved in rocks. Fossilization takes millions of years to happen. If a dinosaur died and was quickly covered in sediment, then the chances of fossilization were high. Once sediment covered the dinosaur's body, the flesh would quickly rot away, but the bones and teeth, the hard parts of the body, would remain. As the sediment gradually built up over the body, minerals from water around the rocks would seep into the bones and they would gradually be turned into rock themselves. Years later, erosion from the wind and water will wear the rock away and expose the dinosaur fossil. With some luck a sharp-eyed fossil collector will find and excavate it. If not, the elements will continue to erode it and it will return to sand or mud.

TYPES OF FOSSIL

Petrified fossils – When the conditions are favourable, minerals seep into the bones and gradually turn the bones into rocks. Petrifaction means 'to turn into a stone'.

Natural mould and cast fossils – Sometimes acidic water dissolves the bone and leaves a hollow space or mould where the bone would have been.

Mummified fossils – These are rarest of fossils, formed when the dinosaur's body has been covered in a dry environment and some of the soft parts have become preserved (mummified) and then fossilized. In these cases, the skin texture and even the folds in it, can be clearly seen.

NOT JUST BONES!

Other parts of dinosaurs were also fossilized, which helps us to understand how they lived and behaved. These include footprints, dung and stomach stones.

DID YOU KNOW?

The word 'fossil' comes from the Latin word 'fossilis' which means 'dug up'.

LOST IN TIME

Palaeontologists estimate that only a few of the dinosaurs that ever lived have been, or will be found as fossils. Most animals did not fossilize. They simply decayed and so are lost from the fossil record.

FOSSIL FACT!

We have known about dinosaur fossils for hundreds of years, but it wasn't until the early 19th century that they were formally recognized as the dinosaurs we learn about today.

WOW, FACT!

Dinosaur fossils have been found on every continent on Earth, including Antarctica!

WHY DID THE DINOSAURS BECOME EXTINCT?

Dinosaurs roamed Earth for more than 150 million years and were the most successful group of animals ever to have lived. They died out 65 million years ago, as did flying reptiles and most sea reptiles. In fact, 70% of all species on Earth died out at the same time, in what is called the K–T Extinction Event. Most scientists blame a combination of a meteorite hitting Earth and massive volcanic eruptions.

GREAT BALLS OF FIRE

When the meteorite hit Earth, it made a huge explosion, causing great destruction. Huge dust clouds blocked the sunlight and caused massive forest fires, storms and tidal waves. The fires wiped out massive areas of plant life. At the same time, volcanoes all over the planet erupted – they poured out red-hot lava (liquid rock) that burned everything it touched.

DARKNESS

After the strike, the dust clouds surrounding Earth shut out sunlight for about six months. It became cold, dusty and dark, making it hard for animals to live and breathe. Without sunlight, plant life died and the herbivores starved, as well as the carnivores that preyed on them.

THE DYING SEA

Underwater volcanoes erupted, sending water from the seabed to the surface. This deep-sea water was low in oxygen and killed most of the plankton living at the surface. The marine reptiles died because some of them fed on plankton and others fed on the plankton-eaters.

DID YOU KNOW?

Snakes, lizards, birds and other small animals survived the K-T Extinction Event, but it is not known why.

DISEASE

As oceans began to dry up, more land bridges appeared. Dinosaurs could walk across these into new areas to look for food. They came into contact with other dinosaurs and passed on diseases to which those dinosaurs had no immunity.

OTHER THEORIES FOR THE DEATH OF THE DINOSAURS INCLUDE:

The climate was cooling. Maybe dinosaurs were unable to adapt to the new conditions. Falling sea levels might have reduced the habitat available to marine and shallow-water dwellers.

Herbivores might have eaten too much of Earth's vegetation and run out of food. They could also have died eating new, poisonous plants that grew in the Cretaceous Period. Without the herbivores, the carnivores would have had nothing to eat and died out, too.

GLOSSARY

ammonite extinct marine molluscs, had coiled shells

ancestor animal from which a later, related animal has evolved

ankylosaurs a group of armoured herbivores that lived 76–68 million years ago

aquatic water-dwelling

archosaurs triassic reptiles, immediate ancestors of the dinosaurs

binocular vision ability to focus on the same thing with two eyes

biped animal that walks on two legs

bipedal walks on two legs

camouflage colouring allowing an animal to blend in with its surroundings

carnivore a meat-eater

cephalopod any mollusc of the class cephalopoda, having tentacles attached to the head, including squid and octopus

ceratopsian plant-eating dinosaurs with horned faces

coelurosaurs 'hollow-tail lizards' – included the most likely ancestors of modern birds

cold-blooded relying on environment to regulate body temperature

conifers evergreen trees and shrubs

Cretaceous last period of the Mesozoic Era, 144–65 million years ago

cycad plant like a palm tree with a middle trunk and leaves

dinosaurs land-dwelling reptiles from the Mesozoic Era

erosion the wearing away of Earth's surface by natural forces

evolution process by which one species changes into another, usually over a long period of time

extinction the process of becoming extinct, no longer existing

femur main thigh bone

fenestrae gap or holes in bone, from the Latin for 'windows'

fern leafy plant growing in damp places

fossil remains preserved in rock

geologist person who studies rocks

grazing feeding on low-growing plants

hadrosaurs duck-billed, plant-eating dinosaurs

hesperornithiformes a group of marine dinosaur

herbivore an animal which just eats plants

horsetail primitive, spore-bearing plant, common in Mesozoic Era

ichthyosaurs sea-dwelling, prehistoric reptiles

Jurassic period of the Mesozoic Era, 206–144 million years ago

K-T Extinction Event extinction event which occurred at the end of the Cretaceous Period, resulting in extinction of the dinosaurs and many other species

lizard scaly-bodied, air-breathing reptile

mammal hairy, warm-blooded animal that nourishes young from mammary glands

membrane thin layer of tissue protecting embryo in egg

Mesozoic Era age of reptiles, 248–65 million years ago, which includes Triassic, Jurassic and Cretaceous Periods

mosasaurs types of marine reptiles

omnivore animal which eats a mixed diet of plants and meat

ornithopods beaked, usually bipedal, plant-eating dinosaurs

orthacanthus a primitive shark

ossicles pea-sized bones

palaeontologist person who studies fossils

Pangaea the 'super-continent' formed of all Earth's land masses

plesiosaurs large marine reptiles that lived in Mesozoic Era

predator animal which hunts other animals to eat

primitive basic, at an early stage of development

pteranodons a group of flying reptiles that were toothless and had a short tail

pterodophytes a type of fern (a plant)

pterosaurs flying, prehistoric reptiles

quadruped animal that walks on four legs

rhynchosaurs herbivorous reptiles from Mezozoic Era

sauropods giant, plant-eating dinosaurs with long neck, small head and long tail

scavenger animal that feeds on (dead) meat which it finds, rather than hunts

scutes bony, protective plates offering defence against attack

semi-bipedal sometimes walks on two legs, at other times walks on four legs

species a category of living things, plants or animals

stegosaurs a group of herbivorous dinosaurs of the Jurassic and early Cretaceous Periods

tendons connect muscle to bone

territory the land or area where an animal lives

theropods fast moving, bipedal carnivores with grasping hands and claws

Triassic first period of the Mesozoic Era, 248–206 million years ago

vertebrae the bones which are linked together to make the spine of an animal

warm-blooded able to keep the body at constant temperature, regardless of the environment

INDEX